ENGLISH
FOR CHINESE SPEAKERS

Textbook Sections

1 Are you crazy?

Intro

✳ Ask these questions to your teacher.

- Is your name Lili/Mingming?
  What's your name?
- Are you Spanish? Where are you from?
- Do you live in Beijing? Where do you live?
- Are there 5 people in your family?
  How many people are there in your family?
- Did you study (major in) marine biology?
  What was your major?
- Do you often play badminton?
  What are your hobbies?
- Do you love eating huoguo (hot pot)?
  What's your favorite food?
- Have you traveled to The Philippines?
  Where have you traveled?

✳ Now ask these questions to your partner and also ask follow-up questions ('Wh' Qs)

Warm-Up

✳ What are Yes/No Questions? When do we ask Yes/No questions? Name as many Yes/No Qs as possible.

- We ask Yes/No questions to determine a simple positive or negative response.
- Are you.../Is it.../Do we.../Does she.../Aren't we.../Isn't she.../Don't you.../Was he.../Were they.../ Did I...? are common Yes/No questions

✳ Elicit an interesting example for each of the common Yes/No Qs above and write them on the board.

1. _____

2. _____

3. _____

4. _____

5. _____

6. _____

7. _____

8. _____

9. _____

10. _____

Now students can open their textbooks and write correct examples from the board in the section above. Then take turns asking and answering these questions with a partner. (ask more follow-up questions)

Are you Chinese? No, I'm not.

你是中国人吗？不，我不是。

Is your teacher good at singing? Yes, she is.

你们老师擅长唱歌吗？是的，她很擅长。

Don't you like pizza? (You don't like pizza?) Yes, I do (like pizza) / No, I don't (like pizza)

你喜欢披萨吗？是的，我喜欢 (披萨)。/ 不，我不喜欢 (披萨)。

Were you excited about coming to class today? Yes, I was.

今天来上课你感到很高兴吗？是的，我很高兴。

Do you like watching movies? Yes, I do

你喜欢看电影吗？是的，我喜欢。

Does orange juice make people healthy? No, it doesn't

橙汁会让人变的健康吗？不，它不会。

Did you take a bus this morning? No, I didn't

你今天早上是做公交车来的吗？不，我没有。

❋ Make (workshop) 3 other Yes/No questions with a partner.

1. _____

2. _____

3. _____

Now change partners and ask these questions and discuss together. (ask more follow-up questions)

✷ Complete these sentences with a partner. Work together. (while speaking out loud)

1. _____ you busy **these days? Why?**

2. _____ your friends like to drink **Qingdao on**
rainy days?

3. You don't want to **go out tonight?** _____,
I do / No, I _____

4. _____ your friend want to **join us for dinner?**

5. _____ you good at **playing pool (pocketball)?**

Now ask these completed questions to your partner
and discuss.

Natural English

✷ Practise the natural English expressions below.

How are you? / How's it going? / How (are) ya goin'/doin'?
Good, thanks / Not bad / Pretty good

What's up? (US/Canada)
Not much / Just the usual

(Are you) alright? (UK)
(I'm) alright

G'day, mate (Aus & NZ)
G'day

Useful Vocabulary

✳ Try to use all of these words in your discussions today. Check them off as you use each one.

Outstanding (杰出的；显著的)   Ridiculous (可笑的；荒谬的)   Annoying (讨厌的；恼人的)

Wonderful (极好的；精彩的)   Grow up (成长)   Adorable (可爱的；可敬重的)

Perfect combination (完美的组合；完美的结合)   Unlimited (无限制的；无限量的)

Classmates (同学)   Leisure time (闲暇时间)

Main Activity

✳ Practise speaking using these questions using the correct grammar. (verb tense)

Ask more follow-up questions (Who/When/Where/Why/What/Which/How…?)

Are/Is/Do/Does…

Aren't you in a good mood today? Why/Why not?

Did you eat doujiang (豆浆) every week in High School? Where? With whom?

Does your mother sometimes drink erguotou (二锅头)? How often/much?

Was there a TV show that you absolutely loved last year? Which one? Why?

Do your neighbors sometimes make a lot of noise? How do you feel about that?

✳ Add 3 relevant and/or common errors from the students' discussion. Correct together on the board.

1. _____

2. _____

3. _____

✳ Please correct these sentences with a partner then check together as a class.

1. Is you confident when you speak in front of other people? _____

2. Are you boring when you watch romantic movies? _____

3. Were you lose your weight? _____

4. Don't your best friend has arbeit? _____

> Take turns asking and answering the corrected questions with a partner.

More Yes/No questions… (Be sure to ask follow-up questions, also.)

Do you have a pet? What kind?

Don't you love having barbecues(烧烤) and beer together?

Were you born in China? Which city/town were you born in?

Aren't you Italian? Where are you from?

Did you enjoy your life when you were in Elementary School? Why/Why not?

> Ask students to provide examples from their discussions using the 'useful vocabulary'.

✳ Add 3 more relevant and/or common errors from the students' discussion. Correct together on the board.

1. _____

2. _____

3. _____

✳ Please correct these sentences with a partner then check together as a class.

5. Are you convenient when you play with your friends? _____

6. Did you cut your hair? _____

7. Is your home nearby to here? _____

8. Do you like a cat? _____

9. Do you know my mind? _____

> Now ask the completed questions above to your partner and discuss.

Critical Thinking & Discussion

1. Introduction: What is a discussion and why do we have them?

Academic discussions form a key part of many university courses, and may also be an important part of your assessment. The skills that you learn through these discussions are also easily transferable to many other areas, such as interviews, presentations and debates.

 Discuss/Debate these topics with your partner or group.

- Do you think your university life is the best time of your life? Why/Why not?

- Is studying hard the most important way to get a good job? Why/Why not?

Review

What did we study today? Please provide three examples with correct responses. Say these correct sentences together as a class.

Preview

Please read through the materials for our next class together. Prepare any questions that you may have and we can discuss them in the warm-up session during the next class.

Have a great day. See you next class!

Goodbye

2 What's going on?

Previous Class Review

✳ What did we do in the previous lesson?
(Yes/No questions) Elicit examples from students of:

- questions & answers
- useful vocabulary

 Write these up on the board and practice them together.

✳ What natural expressions did we work on in the previous class? (How are you?). Ask students for some key examples (prompt/guide them if necessary). Put them on the board and practice saying them correctly together.

Warm-Up

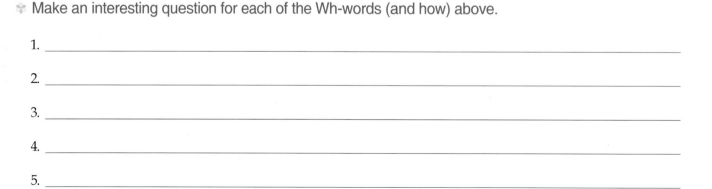

✳ What are Wh-Questions? How many Wh-Question words that you can think of? Why and when do we ask Wh-Questions?

- What, Where, When, Who, Why, Which, How (much/many/ often etc)
- We ask these questions to find out more information about something

✳ Make an interesting question for each of the Wh-words (and how) above.

1. _____
2. _____
3. _____
4. _____
5. _____

6. _____

7. _____

8. _____

9. _____

10. _____

Now students can open their textbooks and write correct examples from the board in the section above. Then take turns asking and answering these questions with a partner. (ask more follow-up questions)

(Things/actions) What is the healthiest food?

(事物/行动)什么是最健康的食物？

(Time) When will you go home?

(时间) 你要什么时候回家？

(Reasons) Why are you studying English?

(理由) 你为什么学习英语？

(Condition/quality) How good is the Chinese soccer team?

(条件/质量) 中国的足球队踢的有多好？

(Amount – uncountable) How much time do we have for the next activity?

(量/不可数的) 我们还有多长时间去准备下一次的比赛呢？

(Amount – countable) How many bottles of Qingdao can you drink?

(量-可数的) 你能喝几瓶青岛？

(Places) Where is the nearest bathroom?

(地点) 最近的桑拿浴在哪里？

(People) Who do you live with?

(人) 你跟谁住在一起？

(Choices) Which city in Korea do you think is the best?

(选择) 你觉得韩国哪个城市最好？

(Frequency) How often do you go swimming?

(频度) 你一般多长时间去游一次泳？

✳ Make 3 other questions with a partner using Wh-Questions.

1. _____

2. _____

3. _____

Ask these questions to your partner and give the correct response.

❋ Complete these sentences with a partner. Work together. (while speaking out loud)

1. _____ do you think is the best genre of music?

2. _____ in the world would you love to visit?

3. _____ does the cherry blossom season start and finish in Korea?

4. _____ is your favorite movie star?

5. _____ do parents stick Chinese red strings out the front of High School's on their kid's University Entrance Exam (Seunul) day?

6. _____ kind of seafood do you enjoy the most?

7. _____ are you feeling today?

8. _____ do you go to a sauna (bathhouse)?

9. _____ homework do you usually do each day?

10. _____ people live in Daejeon?

🎓 Practise speaking using these completed questions with the correct grammar (verb tense).

Useful Vocabulary

❋ Try to use all of these words in your discussions today. Check them off as you use each one.

Fascinating (迷人的)	Good value (质量好的)	Thrilling (特别开心的)
Sensational (引起轰动的)	Hit the books (临时抱佛脚)	Once a year (一年一次)
Refreshing (新鲜的)		

Main Activity

* Ask as many follow-up questions as you can to your partner after they say each of these statements. Take turns. See if you can make 10 different follow-up questions for each statement.

I ate lunch yesterday

I will do something tomorrow

I exercise

I traveled here today

I watch TV

I saw my friend recently

* Add 3 relevant and/or common errors from the students' discussion. Correct together on the board.

1. _____

2. _____

3. _____

* Please correct these sentences with a partner then check together as a class.

1. When do most of people have a free time? _____

2. What height would you like be? _____

3. How do you think about living in Korea? _____

4. I don't know what is the problem. Do you? _____

 After correcting the questions, ask them to a partner. Take turns.

Pronunciation practice

❋ Practise the natural English pronunciation of the highlighted words below.

Light – Right   Collect – Correct   Berry – Belly

I really like to arrive alive after a very long flight in the rain.

The royal lawyer was really loyal to his rural rival.

Try to say this tongue-twister 5 times quickly without making
a mistake – 'Red lorry, yellow lorry'

❋ More discussion questions. (Be sure to ask follow-up questions, also.)

Who do you think is the best dancer in this class?

Why do you think many people visit Korea these days?

How many times have you been to an amusement park?

… How much fun do you usually have when you go there?

Where are you gonna go after this class?

Which local restaurant would you recommend?

How often do you breathe fresh country air?

 Ask students to provide examples from their discussions using the 'useful vocabulary'

❋ Add 3 more relevant and/or common errors from the students' discussion. Correct together.

1. _____

2. _____

3. _____

2. How to prepare for a class discussion

Preparing for your discussion is probably the most important thing that you can do.

Basically, the better your knowledge of the topic to be discussed, the better your chance of successfully contributing to the discussion. Make sure that you go to all your classes, and carefully read any material for the topic. Useful discussions depend on students who have read and thought about the assigned material. Always also try to note any ideas that you feel strongly about.

 Discuss/Debate these topics with your partner or group.

- How big is the generation gap in China these days? Explain
- Who do you admire? Why?

Review

What did we study today? Please provide three examples with correct responses. Say these correct sentences together as a class.

Preview

Please read through the materials for our next class together. Prepare any questions that you may have and we can discuss them in the warm-up session during the next class.

Have a great day. See you next class! BYE BYE

3 How often do you sing to yourself?

Previous Class Review

✻ What did we do in the previous lesson?
(Wh-questions)
Elicit examples from students:

- make questions using as many different
  Wh-words (and how) as possible
- answer these questions together
- use new vocab from the previous class

 Write these up on the board and practice them together.

✻ What pronunciation did we practice last time? ('l' and 'r' sounds). What are some good examples to practice? Say these out loud with a partner to show your perfect pronunciation .

Warm-Up

✻ What are frequency adverbs? Brainstorm some from most to least frequent (often).

- How often ...? asks about the frequency of activities
- Always/almost always/often/sometimes/occasionally/not often/rarely/never are common frequency adverbs

✻ Students should provide some real-world, personalized examples.

1. _____

2. _____

3. _____

 Now students can open their textbooks and write correct examples from the board in the section above. Then take turns asking and answering these questions with a partner. (ask more follow-up questions)

How often do you have rice during dinner? 你经常吃晚饭吗？	I always have rice during dinner (100%) 我一直吃晚饭。
How often do you do your homework? 你经常做作业吗？	I almost always do my homework (95%) 我几乎每次都做作业。
How often do you play computer games? 你经常玩电脑游戏吗？	I often play computer games (80%) 我经常玩电脑游戏。
How often do you tell the truth to your parents? 你经常把真相告诉父母吗？	I sometimes tell the truth to my parents (60%) 有时候我把真相告诉父母。
How often do you go dancing? 你经常去跳舞吗？	I occasionally go dancing (40%) 我偶尔去跳舞。
How often do you ride a bike? 你经常骑自行车吗？	I don't often ride a bike (20%) 我不经常骑自行车。
How often do you study all night? 你经常熬夜学习吗？	I rarely study all night (5%) 我很少熬夜学习
How often do you watch TV shows in English? 你经常看英语电视节目吗？	I never watch TV shows in English (0%) 我从来不看英语电视节目。

Ask the questions above with a partner and give your own answers.

✳ Make 3 other questions with a partner using 'How often …?'

1. _____

2. _____

3. _____

Ask these questions to your partner and give the correct response.

✳ Complete these sentences with a partner. Work together (while speaking out loud)

1. How _____ do you travel to another city/town?

2. I _____ check the daily news. How about you?

3. How often do you _____ drinking games?

Now ask these completed questions to your partner and discuss.

Useful Vocabulary

✤ Try to use all of these words in your discussions today.
Check them off as you use each one.

Heartbroken (悲伤的)	Wide awake (not fast asleep) (完全清醒的)	Scrub (用力擦洗)
Generous (慷慨的)	Regularly (定期的)	Bargain (haggle) (交易)
Exhausted (精疲力竭的)	Grateful (感激的)	Athletic (运动的)
Frustrating (使人沮丧的)		

Main Activity

✤ Practise speaking using these questions using the correct grammar. (verb tense)
Ask more follow-up questions (Who/When/Where/Why/What/Which/How…?)

How often…

do your relatives visit your house?

do you feel disappointed that your class
has finished?

do you play sports?

do you go to a sauna (bathhouse)?

do you thank your mother/father
for preparing food for you?

✽ Add 3 relevant and/or common errors from the students' discussion. Correct together on the board.

1. _____

2. _____

3. _____

✽ Please correct these sentences with a partner then check together as a class.

1. Do you sometimes sing a song to yourself? _____

2. I rarely trip another country. Do you? _____

3. Does you often go to home using public transport? _____

 Now ask the completed questions above to your partner and discuss.

Natural English

✽ Practise the natural English expressions below.

What are you up to (doing now)?   Not much. I'm just watching TV.

Whatcha up to (doing) tonight?   I'm meeting some friends for dinner.

What are ya gonna do this weekend?   Dunno. Maybe just hang out at home.

What did you get up to on the weekend?   Just the usual. I took it pretty easy.

What have you been up to recently?   Same old. Just studying/workin

LETS HANG OUT

Ask these questions to your partner and discuss.

✤ How often do you … (Be sure to ask follow-up questions, also.)

go shopping at a traditional local market?

give presents to your family/friends?

go hiking?

argue with your brother or sister?

sleep for longer than 8 hours?

🎓 Ask students to provide examples from their discussions using the 'useful vocabulary'.

✤ Add 3 more relevant and/or common errors from the students' discussion. Correct together on the board.

1. _____

2. _____

3. _____

✤ Please correct these sentences with a partner then check together as a class.

4. How often are you drunken and overeat? _____

5. How often does you blind date or group meeting? _____

6. How often do you trip to overseas? _____

7. How often do you ask to teacher question _____

 After correcting the sentences. Ask the questions to your partner and discuss.

Critical Thinking & Discussion

3. Giving opinions

Get involved early. An easy way to participate is to add to the existing discussion. Start by making a small contribution like agreeing with someone or asking someone to expand on something that they have said. Remember as well that if you are reluctant to speak before the class, try to say something early in the discussion. The longer you wait, the harder it becomes. Also, if you wait too long, someone else may ask your question or make the comment you intended to make.

- I think (that) …
- I feel (that) …

- I believe (that) …
- In my opinion …

- From what I understand

 Check off each of these expressions after you use them in today's discussion.

Discuss/Debate these topics with your partner or group.

- How often should people eat meat? Why?
- How often should we have national elections? Why?

Review

What did we study today? Please provide three examples with correct responses. Say these correct sentences together as a class.

Preview

Please read through the materials for our next class together. Prepare any questions that you may have and we can discuss them in the warm-up session during the next class.

Have a great day. See you next class! *goodbye!*

4 What will you do on your vacation?

Previous Class Review

❋ What did we do in the previous lesson?
(How often …?) Elicit examples from students of:

- common questions
- natural responses/relevant vocab

❋ Write these up on the board and practice them together.

 What natural expressions did we work on in the previous class? (What are you up to?). Ask students for some key examples (prompt/guide them if necessary). Put them on the board and practice saying them correctly together..

Warm-Up

❋ When do we use 'will/won't', 'probably will/won't', 'might'? Give some examples.

- Talking about future actions that are not 100% definite
- Used to show predictions, intentions, assumptions (hopes), arrangements

❋ Students should brainstorm some real-world, personalized examples.

1. _____

2. _____

3. _____

 Now students can open their textbooks and write correct examples from the board in the section above. Then take turns asking and answering these questions with a partner. (ask more follow-up questions)

Predictions 预测	My friend will become a teacher when she's older. 当我朋友长大了，将会成为一名教师。
Intentions 意向	I probably won't drink too much tonight. 我今晚可能不会喝太多。
Assumptions/hopes 假定/希望	My boyfriend might buy me a present for my birthday. 说不定我男朋友会给我买生日礼物。
Conditions 条件	If it rains tomorrow, I won't play tennis. 明天下雨的话，我就不打网球。
Arrangements 准备	I will meet my sister after class. (Definite – I'm going to meet…) 上课之后我要见妹妹。（明确的 – 我要去见…）

✷ Workshop 3 other questions with a partner using 'will'.

1. _____

2. _____

3. _____

Ask these questions to your partner and give the correct response.

✷ Complete these sentences with a partner. Work together. (while speaking out loud

1. How _____ you celebrate after you finish your exams?

2. _____ will your family do for the next ZhongQiu holidays?

3. Will you _____ a book today?

4. What time will you probably _____ home today?

5. Will you _____ dinner with your parents tonight?

6. Which team _____ win the next Soccer (Football) World Cup? _____ might be the star player?

 Now ask these completed questions to your partner and discuss.

Useful Vocabulary

❋ Try to use all of these words in your discussions today. Check them off as you use each one.

Morning routine (早晨的日常工作)	Emigrate (移居国外)	Bachelorette (未婚女子)
Elective (选修科目)	Entertainer (表演者)	Stadium (体育场)
Addicted to (对。。有瘾)	Integrate/assimilate (成为一体)	
Humid (muggy/sweaty/steamy) (潮湿的)		Space travel (宇宙旅行)
Leisure time (闲暇时间)		

Main Activity

❋ Practise speaking by answering these questions using the correct grammar (verb tense).

Ask more follow-up questions (Who/When/Where/Why/What/Which/How…?)

Will…

Do you think you'll (you will) be living in the same place in 2 years (from now)?

Will you watch a TV show or movie in English this week?

Do you think you might be famous one day?

Will you live in another country sometime in the future?

Which subjects will you probably study next semester?

✳ Add 3 relevant and/or common errors from the students' discussion. Correct together on the board.

1. _____

2. _____

3. _____

✳ Please correct these sentences with a partner then check together as a class.

1. Will you meeting your friends tonight? _____

2. Will you probably graduate your university 3 months later? _____

3. When might you make a girlfriend/boyfriend? _____

4. Will you be go to the library after class? _____

 Now ask the corrected questions to your partner and discuss.

Pronunciation practice

✳ Practise the natural English pronunciation of the highlighted words below.

What's the hardest thing about the English language?

Where's the best place to buy a cheese sandwich around here?

In which months do you wear warm clothes?

Did you see the strange message on the fridge under the bridge?

 Now take turns asking these questions to your partner and discuss.

❋ More discussion questions… (Be sure to ask follow-up questions, also.)

When will you go to watch a live sporting game?

What do you think the weather will probably be like tomorrow?

When will you get married?

Do you think humans will ever live on another planet?

When might you next eat kimbap?

> 🎓 Ask students to provide examples from their discussions using the 'useful vocabulary'.

❋ Add 3 more relevant and/or common errors from the students' discussion. Correct together and leave the sentences on the board.

1. _____

2. _____

3. _____

❋ Please correct these sentences with a partner then check together as a class.

5. Do you think your friend will marry with his girlfriend?

_____

6. Where will you probably play with your friends on the weekend?

_____

7. Will you absent class tomorrow? _____

8. Where might you go to vacation next summer? _____

> 🎓 Now ask the corrected questions to your partner and discuss.

4. Observing and listening:

Observing

When you are taking part in tutorial discussions, try to observe how other students participate. Watch how the other participants ask questions, how they disagree or support things being said, how they clarify things, how they give their own opinions and how long and often they speak.

Listening

"If we were supposed to talk more than we listen, we would have two tongues and one ear." Mark Twain

Listening is an essential skill and an important element of any discussion. Indeed it can be said that listening is the key to all communication. Listening is not a passive activity, and competent listeners don't just hear what is being said, rather they think about it and actively process it.

- being attentive and focused
- listening with an open mind and evaluating what is said

 Check off these skills as you achieve them during today's discussion.

Discuss/Debate these topics with your partner or group.

- What do you think will be the most influential new technologies in the future?
- How will the world's different cultural identities be affected by increasing globalization?

Review

What did we study today? Please provide three examples with correct responses. Say these correct sentences together as a class.

Preview

Please read through the materials for our next class together. Prepare any questions that you may have and we can discuss them in the warm-up session during the next clas.

Have a great day. See you next class!

5 Do you want to go home?

Previous Class Review

❋ What did we do in the previous lesson?
(will) Give examples of:

- common questions
- natural responses
- relevant vocab

❋ Write these up on the board and practice them together.

 What pronunciation did we work on in the previous class? (English Language/months). Write some key examples on the board and practice saying them correctly together.

Warm-Up

❋ When do we use 'want'? Elicit the relevant grammar. When is it used?

- 'Want' is used to express wish or desire

❋ Brainstorm some real-world, personalized examples from students (to be written on the board).

1. _____

2. _____

3. _____

 Now students can open their textbooks and write correct examples from the board in the section above. Then take turns asking and answering these questions with a partner. (ask more follow-up questions)

Language Focus

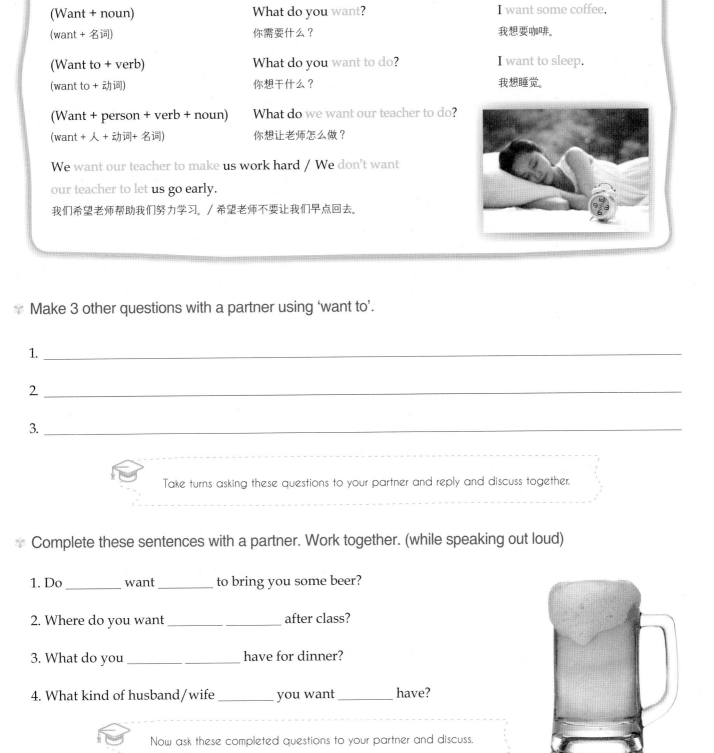

(Want + noun)

(want + 名词)

What do you want?

你需要什么？

I want some coffee.

我想要咖啡。

(Want to + verb)

(want to + 动词)

What do you want to do?

你想干什么？

I want to sleep.

我想睡觉。

(Want + person + verb + noun)

(want + 人 + 动词 + 名词)

What do we want our teacher to do?

你想让老师怎么做？

We want our teacher to make us work hard / We don't want our teacher to let us go early.

我们希望老师帮助我们努力学习。/ 希望老师不要让我们早点回去。

✴ Make 3 other questions with a partner using 'want to'.

1. _____

2. _____

3. _____

Take turns asking these questions to your partner and reply and discuss together.

✴ Complete these sentences with a partner. Work together. (while speaking out loud)

1. Do _____ want _____ to bring you some beer?

2. Where do you want _____ _____ after class?

3. What do you _____ _____ have for dinner?

4. What kind of husband/wife _____ you want _____ have?

Now ask these completed questions to your partner and discuss.

Natural English

✳ Practise the natural English expressions below.

Do ya wanna speak more natural English? (Do you want to...?)

Whaddaya want? (What do you want?)   I want some coffee/I wanna coffee (I want a coffee)

Whaddaya wanna do? (What do you want to do?)   I wanna sleep (I want to sleep).

Whadda we want our teacher to do? (What do we want...)   We want.../We don't want...

Useful Vocabulary

✳ Try to use all of these words in your discussions today. Check them off as you use each one.

A pushover (容易打败的人)	Courageous (勇敢的)	Embarrassing (尴尬的)
Hard-working (勤勉地)	Bizarre (奇怪的/奇特的)	Unstoppable (无法停止的)
Freezing/Boiling (冰冻的/炎热的)	Coward (胆小鬼)	A nightmare (噩梦)
Relentless (坚韧的)		

Main Activity

✳ Practise speaking using these questions.

Ask more follow-up questions (Who/When/Where/Why/What/Which/How...?)

Do you want/Do ya wanna...?

your parents to give you more money?

(to) never have to work again in your life?

(to) be famous?

(a) bunch of roses to be delivered to you right now? From whom?

(to) travel to every single country in the world? Why/Why not?

* Add 3 relevant and/or common errors from the students' discussion. Correct together on the board.

1. _____

2. _____

3. _____

* Please correct these sentences together with a partner then check together as a class.

1. Do you want live in the country? _____

2. Don't you want brother to remain single for his whole life? _____

3. Do want to see alien life arrive on earth? _____

4. Do you want to play bowling this weekend? _____

 Now ask the completed questions above to your partner and discuss.

More discussion questions (Be sure to ask follow-up questions, also.)

Do you want me to stand up and act like a chicken?

I don't want this class to ever end. How about you?

Do you want to/(Do ya wanna) turn the air-con up or down?

Don't you sometimes want to tell your parents exactly what you think?

Do you want to/(Do ya wanna) be powerful?

 Ask students to provide examples from their discussions using the 'useful vocabulary'.

✳ Write 3 more relevant and/or common errors from the students' discussion (on the board). Correct together.

1. _____

2. _____

3. _____

✳ Please correct these sentences with a partner then check together as a class.

5. Do you want listening the music? _____

6. How many money do you want to make? _____

7. Do you want to climb the mountains after class? _____

8. Do you want to go to shopping later? _____

9. Do you wanna chicken? _____

> Take turns asking and answering the corrected questions with a partner.

Critical Thinking & Discussion

5. Some skills that will help you to become a better listener include:

- Relax, focus on the speaker and clear your mind of distractions.

- Help the speaker to feel at ease. Nod or use other gestures or words to encourage them to continue.

- Maintain eye contact but don't stare – show you are listening and understanding what is being said.

- Be an active listener and don't let your attention drift. Stay attentive and focus on what is being said.

- Identify the main ideas being discussed.

- Evaluate what is being said. Think about how it relates to the main idea/theme of the discussion.

- Listen with an open mind and be receptive to new ideas and points of view.

- Avoid prejudice and stay impartial.

- Test your understanding; try to mentally paraphrase what is being said.

- Wait and watch for non-verbal communication - gestures, facial expressions, and eye-movements can all be important.

 Check off these skills as you practice them during today's discussion.

Discuss/Debate these topics with your partner or group

- Do you want to meet a world leader? Who would you choose to meet? What questions would you ask them? Why?
- Do you want to be in a popular movie? Why/Why not?

Review

What did we study today? Please provide three examples with correct responses. Say these correct sentences together as a class.

Preview

Please read through the materials for our next class. Prepare any questions that you may have and we can discuss them in the warm-up session during the next class.

Have a great day. See you next class!

6 Mmm, this is tasty!

Previous Class Review

❋ What did we do in the previous 5 units?
  Elicit 1 or 2 examples from each unit of:

  • common questions, responses, vocab

❋ Write these up on the board and practice them together.

 What pronunciation and natural expressions did we work on in the previous 5 units? Ask students for a key example from each unit. Put them on the board and practice saying them correctly together..

❋ Practice these together with a partner for a few minutes.

Language Focus

Is it tasty?   Delicious

(Yeah, it's.../No, it's...)   Excellent / Great

How is it?   Good / Quite tasty

(What does it taste like? It's...)   Not bad / Pretty good

                                      Not great / Not so good

                                      Pretty bad / Terrible

                                      Disgusting

✹ Look at the pictures of food above. Ask your partner about the taste of each one and take turns answering – Do you think _____ is/are tasty?

✹ Complete these sentences with a partner. Work together (while speaking out loud).

1. How _____ do you eat fried rice. (炒饭)?

2. What _____ you have for dinner tonight?

3. What do you _____ to drink when you eat chicken?

 Now ask these completed questions to your partner and discuss.

Useful Vocabulary

❋ Try to use all of these words in your discussions today. Check them off as you use each one.

All-you-can-eat (所有你能吃的)	Starving (饥饿)	Complimentary (赠送的)
Gourmet (美食家)	Bloated (浮肿的)	Pig out (狼吞虎咽)
Fatty (油腻的)	Once in a blue moon (百年不遇)	Nutritious (有营养的)
Hectic (繁忙的)	A great cook (一个伟大的厨师)	Cafeteria (自助餐厅)
Live by myself (自己一个人住)	Herbs and spices (药草和香料)	Best in the universe (全宇宙最好的)

Main Activity

❋ Practise asking and answering these questions using the correct grammar.

Ask more follow-up questions (Who/When/Where/Why/What/Which/How…?)

Where do you usually eat lunch?

Is samgyeopsal your favourite food?

Who do you think is the best cook in the world?

How often does your father cook?

Which restaurant do you really want to eat at?

Are you hungry now?

❋ Add 3 relevant and/or common errors from the students' discussion.
Correct together and leave the corrected sentences on the board.

1. _____

2. _____

3. _____

* Please correct these sentences with a partner then check together as a class.

1. How many times have you overeaten when you were drunken?

_____

2. How do you think about having pizza for breakfast?

_____

3. Does one of your friends want to lose his weight?

_____

4. How often do you have an appointment with your sister?

_____

 Take turns asking and answering the corrected questions with a partner.

Natural Expressions/Pronunciation Practice

* Practise the natural English expressions and pronunciation below.

How are you? Not bad / Pretty good

Do you really like to run in the light rain?

What are you up to? Not much.

Have you ever dropped a cheese sandwich on your clothes?

Whaddaya gonna do this weekend? Dunno. Maybe just hang out at home.

More Discussion Questions: (Be sure to ask follow-up questions, also.)

How often do you get food delivered?

What's your favourite Korean/
international food?

Which fast food do you think is the best/
healthiest?

Will you eat out or at home tonight?

How much do you usually eat when you
go to a buffet restaurant?

Do you think you'll skip breakfast tomorrow morning?

How often do you have junk food?

Do you usually want to have dessert after dinner?

 Ask students to provide examples from their discussions
using the 'useful vocabulary'.

❋ Write 3 more relevant and/or common errors from the students' discussion (on the board). Then
correct them together.

1. _____

2. _____

3. _____

❋ Please correct these sentences with a partner then check together as a class.

5. Will eating a lot of meat make kid's height bigger? _____

6. What do you want to eating when you are hungover (sukjae issoyo)?

_____

7. When will you not eat during more than 12 hours? _____

8. Is there a McDonalds nearby to here? _____

9. What's your favorite menu at a Chinese restaurant?

_____

 Take turns asking and answering the corrected questions with a partner.

Presentation Topics

❋ Choose one of these topics and prepare a short presentation with a partner/partners.

- Is your life easy or difficult these days? Why?

- What do you think will be the biggest changes in the world in the next 15 years?

- How often do you think people should give money to charity? Why?

- What country do you really want to visit? Why?

- Why do you think so many people visit Korea these days?

Preview

Please read through the materials for our next class. Prepare any questions that you may have and we can discuss them in the warm-up session during the next class.

Have a great day. See you next class!

7 | What are you thinking about?

Previous Class Review

❋ What did we do in the previous lesson? (want to)
Give examples of:

- common questions
- natural responses
- relevant vocab

❋ Write these up on the board and practice them together.
What pronunciation did we work on in the previous
class? (Whaddaya wanna…?). Write some
key examples on the board and practice saying them correctly together.

 Practice these together with a partner for a few minutes.

Warm-Up

❋ When do we use the Present Continuous? Elicit the relevant grammar.

The Present Continuous is 'Subject + 'to be' + verb-ing'. It is used to describe:

- actions which are happening at the moment of speaking
- a temporary event or situation
- and emphasize a continuing series of repeated actions (with always, constantly, forever)
- fixed plans in the near future

❋ Elicit some real-world, personalized examples from students (to be written on the board).

1. _____

2. _____

3. _____

Now students can open their textbooks and write correct examples from the board in the section above.
Then take turns asking and answering these questions with a partner. (ask more follow-up questions)

Language Focus

(Happening now) (现在发生的)	We are studying the Present Continuous. 我们现在学习现在进行时
(Temporary) (临时性的)	Is it raining? Yes, it is. / No, it isn't. / No, it's not. 现在下雨吗？ 是/不是
(Repeated actions) (反复性的行动)	My parents are always telling me to study harder/come home earlier. 我的父母一直告诉我要更加努力学习/早点回家。
(Fixed future plans) (确实的未来计划)	I'm meeting my friends tonight. 今天晚上我要跟朋友见面

✼ Make 3 other questions with a partner using the 'want to'.

1. _____

2. _____

3. _____

🎓 Take turns asking these questions to your partner and reply and discuss together.

✼ Complete these sentences with a partner. Work together. (while speaking out loud)

1. What _____ you doing right now?

2. Who do you know that is _____ complaining?

3. What other subjects are _____ studying these days?

4. Where are you _____ immediately after class?

🎓 Now ask these completed questions to your partner and discuss.

Useful Vocabulary

✳ Try to use all of these words in your discussions today. Check them off as you use each one.

Downtime (休息时间)

High-maintenance (细心的)

Tardy (晚的)

Committed (忠诚的)

Slam dunk (扣篮)

Walking distance (步行距离)

Kick back (踢回)

Cold snap (寒流)

Wandering around (四处游荡)

Blowing in the wind (随风飘荡)

Slim (苗条的)

Main Activity

✳ Practise speaking using these questions using the correct grammar.

Ask more follow-up questions (Who/When/Where/Why/What/Which/How…?)

What do you think YaoMing is doing at the moment?

Are you reading a book these days?

Who is constantly coming late to class?

How many people do you think are sending a Kakao Talk message right now?

Look out the window! What's happening?

✳ Add 3 relevant and/or common errors from the students' discussion. Correct together on the board.

1. _____

2. _____

3. _____

✻ Please correct these sentences with a partner then check together as a class.

1. Do you working on an assignment at the moment?

_____

2. Are you still work at your part-time job?

_____

3. Why do you forever arguing at me?

_____

4. What sort of music are teenagers listening to this days?

_____

5. I'm thinking to contact G-Dragon. Should I?

_____

 Take turns asking and answering the corrected questions with a partner.

Pronunciation practice

✻ Practise the natural English pronunciation of the highlighted words below.

They – Day   There – Dare   Those – Doze   Worthy – Wordy   Breathe - Breed

Would they bathe there on another day, in rather unworthy weather, though?

Would you rather your father or mother dare the other to wear leather?

The question is whether to bother to breathe these worthy words or whether you'd rather doze.

Do you want this, that, or the other? Those are your options.

More Yes/No questions… (Be sure to ask follow-up questions, also.)

Are you visiting your relatives this weekend?

Why are more and more people becoming vegetarians these days?

Are you going to a café this afternoon?

Is it snowing now?

Are you playing basketball with your friends after this class?

🎓 Ask students to provide examples from their discussions using the 'useful vocabulary'.

❋ Write 3 more relevant and/or common errors from the students' discussion (on the board). Correct together.

1. _____

2. _____

3. _____

❋ Please correct these sentences with a partner then check together as a class.

6. What are you wear? _____

7. These days, more people is using Wechat than phone texting? Do you agree?

_____

8. Do you think your English is improve? _____

9. Why do you always smiling? _____

10. What will you doing on the weekend? _____

 Take turns asking and answering the corrected questions with a partner.

Critical Thinking & Discussion

6. Asking for opinions

- What do you think?
- What's your opinion?
- How do you feel about it?
- Would you agree with that?
- Any comments?
- What are your views on …?
- How about you?
- Is there anything you'd like to add?

 Check off these questions after using them during today's discussion.

Discuss/Debate these topics with your partner or group.

- These days, more people are getting their news online.
  What are the pros and cons of this?
- Why is the climate changing so rapidly these days?

Review

What did we study today? Please provide three examples with correct responses. Say these correct sentences together as a class.

Preview

Please read through the materials for our next class. Prepare any questions that you may have and we can discuss them in the warm-up session during the next class.

Have a great day. See you next class!

Previous Class Review

✳ What did we do in the previous lesson?
(Present Continuous)
Elicit examples from students of:

- common questions
- natural responses
- relevant vocab

✳ Write these up on the board and practice them together.
What pronunciation did we work on in the previous
class? (they - day).
Write some key examples on the board and practice
saying them correctly together.

 Practice these together with a partner for a few minutes.

Warm-Up

✳ When do we use the Simple Past? Elicit the relevant grammar and write in on the board.

- The Simple Past is used to talk about a completed action in a time before now.
- The time of the action can be in the recent past or the distant past and the action duration is not important.

✳ Elicit an interesting example for each of the common Yes/No Qs above and write them on the board.

1. _____

2. _____

3. _____

 Now students can open their textbooks and write correct examples from the board in the section above.
Then take turns asking and answering these questions with a partner. (ask more follow-up questions)

Language Focus

Regular 定期的	I played the piano when I was in Elementary School. 我上小学的时候弹钢琴了。	
Question 疑问	Did you live in Seoul when you were young? 小时候住在首尔吗？	Yes, I did. / No, I didn't. 是，住在首尔 /不, 没住在首尔
Negative 否定	I didn't drink coffee this morning. 今天早上我没喝咖啡。	
Irregular 不定期的	I went home late last night. / I sat in front of my computer all day yesterday. 昨天晚上很晚才回家。 / 昨天一直坐在电脑前面	
To be	Were you shy when you were younger? 小时候你很害羞嘛？ 是/没有	Yes, I was. / No, I wasn't.
动词	Was he in this class last month? 上个月那个男的也听过这门课吗？	

✳ Make 3 other questions with a partner using the Simple Past.

1. _____

2. _____

3. _____

Take turns asking these questions to your partner and reply and discuss together.

✳ Complete these sentences with a partner. Work together (while speaking out loud).

1. My brother _____ TV for 5 hours straight yesterday?

2. _____ you buy anything on the weekend?

3. Did you _____ how to swim when you were 10 years old?

4. _____ you awake at midnight last night?

Now ask these completed questions to your partner and discuss.

Useful Vocabulary

❋ Try to use all of these words in your discussions today. Check them off as you use each one.

French kiss (舌吻)	Peck on the cheek (亲吻脸颊)	Awesome (令人惊叹的)
Stuffed my face (饱的)	Weekend trip (周末旅行)	Concentrate on (集中注意)
Fried an egg (炒鸡蛋)	Text messages (短信)	Model student (模范学生)
Stuffed (塞住)	Lightning fast (迅速的)	Impatient (不耐烦的)

Main Activity

❋ Practise speaking using these questions using the correct grammar.

Ask more follow-up questions (Who/When/Where/Why/What/Which/How…?)

Did you…?

eat breakfast this morning?

travel overseas last summer?

have a part-time job last year?

go to a nightclub (dance club) before you were 20?

cook something for yourself last week?

kiss someone yesterday?

❋ Add 3 relevant and/or common errors from the students' discussion. Correct together and leave the corrected sentences on the board.

1. _____

2. _____

3. _____

✷ Please correct these sentences with a partner then check together as a class.

1. Did you looked at the subway timetable this morning? _____

2. What time did you came back to home last night? _____

3. Do you played Starcraft when you were young? _____

4. When's the last time you swimmed in the ocean? _____

5. Do you catch a cold? _____

> 🎓 Now take turns asking and answering the corrected questions with your partner.

More Discussion Questions: (Be sure to ask follow-up questions, also.)

Was your dad a fast runner when he was young?

What movie did you see recently? Did you like it?

Did you have breakfast/lunch/dinner before class?

Who was the last person that you called (on your phone)?

How long did you wait for the subway/bus this morning? Or did you drive or walk here?

✷ Write 3 more relevant and/or common errors from the students' discussion (on the board). Then correct them together.

1. _____

2. _____

3. _____

✳ Please correct these sentences with a partner then check together as a class.

6. Did you ate NiuRoumian (牛肉面) yesterday? _____

7. Was you drunken last night? _____

8. Did you overeat and your film was cut? _____

9. Do you play yoga in 2016? _____

10. What did you do on last weekend? _____

11. I met her two weeks before _____

> 🎓 Take turns asking and answering the corrected questions with a partner.

Natural Expressions

✳ Practice the natural English expressions below.

> See ya later.   Yeah, take it easy   Have a good one.   Thanks, you too.

Critical Thinking & Discussion

7. There are good ways and bad ways to ask other people for their ideas or opinions.

Good question types will encourage valuable answers, reveal information and stimulate conversation

They include: open-ended questions that require longer more detailed answers (such as 'Could you tell me what you think about this?'; probing questions that require deep answers (such as 'How exactly did you feel on that day?'); hypothetical questions (such as 'What would you do if the university was suddenly closed?'); and devil's advocate type questions which are often challenging people's natural opinions (such as 'Pak Kun Hye shouldn't have been impeached, don't you agree?').

Bad question types are predictive or ask only for simple answers, which have a negative impact on the flow of a discussion.

They include: closed questions where the respondent has little chance to elaborate and need only provide a 'yes/no' type answer (such as 'Are you bad at taking exams?'). It needs to be noted though that these type of questions can sometimes be useful, such as to quickly check facts or confirm something; leading questions, which predict an answer (such as 'You are bad at taking math, aren't you?'; and negative or aggressive questions, which make a respondent less likely to want to answer.

Workshop some:

- Open-ended Qs
- Probing Qs
- Hypothetical Qs
- Devil's advocate Qs

together and write them up on the board.

 Check off each of these styles of question after using them in today's discussion.

❋ Discuss/Debate these topics with your partner or group

- Did you have a pet when you were growing up? What attitudes and abilities did this help you develop?
- Were you a good student in High School? Why/Why not?

Review

What did we study today? Please provide three examples with correct responses. Say these correct sentences together as a class.

Preview

Please read through the materials for our next class together. Prepare any questions that you may have and we can discuss them in the warm-up session during the next class.

Have a great day. See you next class! See Ya Later

9 | Take it easy!

Previous Class Review

❋ What did we do in the previous lesson?
(Simple past)
Elicit examples from students of:

- common questions
- natural responses
- relevant vocab

❋ Write these up on the board and practice them together.
What natural expressions did we work on in the previous class? (See ya later!). Ask students for some key examples (prompt/guide them if necessary). Put them on the board and practice saying them correctly together.

 Practice these together with a partner for a few minutes.

Warm-Up

❋ When do we use 'Imperatives'? Brainstorm the relevant grammar and write in on the board.

- 'Imperatives' are used to express orders, instructions, directions, warnings, advice & requests

❋ Brainstorm real-world, personalized examples for each one from students (to be written on the board).

1. _____

2. _____

3. _____

4. _____

5. _____

6. _____

🎓 Now students can open their textbooks and write correct examples from the board in the section above. Then take turns asking and answering these questions with a partner. (ask more follow-up questions)

Language Focus

(Orders) (命令)	Get out! 出去!	(Instructions) (指示)	Open your books! 打开你的书!
(Directions) (指点)	Keep on going! 继续走!	(Warnings) (警告)	Look out! / Be careful! 小心! / 小心点!
(Advice) (忠告)	Eat more fruit! / Don't smoke! 多吃点水果! / 不要抽烟!	(Requests) (要求)	Help me, please! 请帮帮我!

✳ Make (workshop) 3 other statements with a partner using 'Imperatives'.

1. _____

2. _____

3. _____

🎓 Take turns saying these statements to your partner and discuss together.

Useful Vocabulary

❋ Try to use all of these words in your discussions today. Check them off as you use each one.

Sit up straight (坐直)	Please be kind (亲切点)	Turn around and go back (回去)
Don't lie (别说谎)	Talk to me (跟我说)	Look me in the eye (看看我)
Work with me (跟我工作)	Hang in there (再等等)	Stop complaining (别抱怨)
Never give up (别放弃)	Tell me something interesting (告诉我一些有趣的事)	
Shut up (闭嘴)		

 Imagine you are the military leader of your partner. Order them around for 1 minute. Now change roles.

You are now an extremely kind and wise life counsellor. Give good advice for a happy and healthy life. Take turns.

Now your partner is going to jog to your house. Give them directions (door to door). Switch.

Main Activity

❋ Practise sasking and answering these questions using the correct grammar.

Ask more follow-up questions (Who/When/Where/Why/What/Which/How...?)

Just do it!

'Always look on the bright side of life!' Are you good at doing this? When?

'Drink more alcohol!' Is this good advice? Why/Why not?

'Don't work too hard!' Have your parents ever said this to you? How often?

'Sit down and shut up!' Who would you like to say this to? (except your teacher, of course)

'Let's party!' When you was the last time you heard this? The next time?

✳ Add 3 relevant and/or common errors from the students' discussion. Correct together and leave the corrected sentences on the board.

1. _____

2. _____

3. _____

✳ When giving instructions and directions, it's good to identify the order of actions:

First, go to a convenience store. Then, open a fridge and grab a beer. Next, pay for it. After that, go outside and find a comfortable place to sit down. Finally, drink it.

Tell your partner how to:

Start a car   Buy perfume   Take a soccer penalty kick
Prepare cup ramyeon

Take turns   Think of your own examples and ask your partner!

Pronunciation practice

✳ Practise the natural English pronunciation of the highlighted words below.

Face – Pace   Fair – Pair   Firm – Perm   Fresher – Pressure   Fries – Prize

Faint – Paint   Fart – Part   Fashion – Passion   Four – Pour   Fork – Pork   Phrase – Praise

Laugh – lap   Referee (Ref) – Rep   Whiff – whip   Hof – Hop   Enough – In up

Is it fair to praise the phrase, 'A firm perm shows a passion for fashion!'?

Are four fries enough of a prize if you pour paint on a ref's face and make him faint?

There's pressure to make the air fresher after a whiff of a fart makes you laugh.

More Discussion Questions: (Be sure to ask follow-up questions, also.)

'Gimme (Give me) a break!' When have you wanted to say this?

Where's a good café near here? Tell your partner how to get there.

What would you say to a young child who is about to cross a very busy road?

Everything your partner does makes you upset. Tell them. (Don't look at me!/Stop holding your pen! etc)

Recommend good things to do/not do if you travel to the U.S.?

Ask students to provide examples from their discussions using the 'useful vocabulary'.

✷ Write 3 more relevant and/or common errors from the students' discussion (on the board). Then correct them together.

1. _____

2. _____

3. _____

✷ Please correct these sentences with a partner then check together as a class.

1. Eat medicine! _____

2. Drink more fastly! _____

3. Borrow me W10,000, please. _____

4. Listen your mother! _____

5. Don't teasing me! _____

6. Go to home! _____

7. Careful not do mistake. _____

8. Always do best! _____

9. See you again! _____

10. I dropped my phone into the toilet. What a stupid! _____

11. Frankly speaking, please write your sign on this print! _____

Take turns saying the corrected statements with a partner.

Critical Thinking & Discussion

8. Agreeing

- Absolutely!
- I totally agree.
- I know exactly what you mean.
- That's a good point.
- That's true.
- I'm with you on that.
- I take your point.
- That's a great idea.
- I couldn't agree more.
- You're quite right.

 Check off each of these expressions after using them in today's discussion.

✳ Discuss/Debate these topics with your partner or group

- Live your life to its fullest! (Seize the day! / Carpe diem!). Why is this good/bad advice?
- Be a better person! How can you achieve this?

Review

What did we study today? Please provide three examples with correct responses. Say these correct sentences together as a class.

Preview

Please read through the materials for our next class. Prepare any questions that you may have and we can discuss them in the warm-up session during the next class.

Have a great day. See you next class!

10 What are you gonna do tonight?

Previous Class Review

✳ What did we do in the previous lesson?
(at, on, in)
Elicit examples from students of:

- common statement/questions
- natural responses
- relevant vocab

✳ Write these up on the board and practice them together.
What pronunciation did we work on in the previous class? (Imperatives). Ask students for some key examples. Put them on the board and practice saying them correctly together.

 Practice these together with a partner for a few minutes.

Warm-Up

✳ When do we use 'going to'? Elicit the relevant grammar and write in on the board.

'Going to' is used to describe:

- intentions (planned actions)
- confident predictions (based on evidence)

✳ Brainstorm some real-world, personalized examples from students (to be written on the board).

1. _____

2. _____

3. _____

 Now students can open their textbooks and write correct examples from the board in the section above. Then take turns asking and answering these questions with a partner. (ask more follow-up questions)

Language Focus

Form:	to be + going to + infinitive
Function:	
Intentions:	I'm (not) going to meet my friend for coffee after class.
	我（不）会在课后与朋友见面喝咖啡。
	Are you going to eat Hotpot (火锅) when you visit Chengdu on?
	你去成都旅游时，你会去吃火锅吗？
Confident predictions:	That kid is (isn't) going to be a professional ballet dancer when he gets older.
	那个孩子长大后（不）会成为一名专业的芭蕾舞演员。

FC Seoul are 2 goals behind with 1 minute left. They're going to lose/They're not going to win.

FC首尔在比赛还剩1分钟时进2球。他们不会赢。

❋ Make 3 other questions with a partner using 'going to'.

1. _____

2. _____

3. _____

Take turns asking these questions to your partner and reply and discuss together.

❋ Complete these sentences with a partner. Work together. (while speaking out loud)

1. Are you _____ to play badminton this evening?

2. After I retire, I'm going _____ live in the countryside. How about you?

3. Are you going to _____ a hard time sleeping tonight after drinking 3 coffees?

4. I'm so tired. I think I'm going to _____ to bed early tonight. You?

Now ask these completed questions to your partner and discuss.

Natural English

❋ Practise the natural English expressions below. (Make/Do)

Whatcha gonna do tonight? (What are you going to...?) I'm just gonna hang out at home. (I'm just going to...)

Where are ya gonna go after class? / Where are ya going after class?   (Where are you going to go...)

I'm gonna go da a café with a friend.   (I'm going to go to...)

Get: When are ya gonna get a taxi (take/catch) / present (receive) /job (obtain)? When does it get (become) dark these days? When d'ya think ya gonna get (arrive/return) home tonight? Get (bring/ grab) your stuff (things)! Let's get outta here (go/leave)!

Make: You're gonna make mistakes, so don't worry about it!   Do ya wanna make (earn) a lot of money? Why?

Do: Are ya gonna do yoga/some exercise/your homework/some housework (chores) tonight?

 Brainstorm some other natural examples of 'get', 'make', and 'do' with your teacher and discuss.

Useful Vocabulary

❋ Try to use all of these words in your discussions today. Check them off as you use each one.

Punctual (准时的)	Go on a diet (开始减肥)	Ludicrous (可笑的)
Conscientious (认真负责的)	Put my feet up (休息)	Considerate (体贴的)
Dye my hair (染头发)	Overcrowded (挤满的)	Let her know (告诉她)
Hair salon (美发廊)	Sharp (锋利的)	Pouring (倾泻)

Main Activity

✳ Practise asking and answering these questions using the correct grammar.

Ask more follow-up questions (Who/When/
    Where/Why/What/Which/How…?)

Are you going to study or relax tonight?

Why is/isn't your teacher gonna wear a pink
dress tomorrow?

How are you going to be nicer to your parents as
you get older?

Are you gonna work harder next class?

Where are you gonna go swimming when you
go to Busan?

✳ Add 3 relevant and/or common errors from the students' discussion. Correct together and leave the
corrected sentences on the board.

1. _____

2. _____

3. _____

✳ Please correct these sentences with a partner then check together as a class.

1. Are you going to cut your hair soon? _____

2. Who are/aren't you gonna go to dancing with (in Hongdae/Gangnam etc) this Friday night?

   _____

3. Are you gonna review this lesson to home tonight? _____

4. Which famous restaurant are you gonna go to this month? _____

5. Why are we gonna Dutch pay for dinner tonight? _____

> Take turns asking and answering the corrected questions with a partner.

More Discussion Questions: (Be sure to ask follow-up questions, also.)

Are you ever gonna give up (eating) chocolate?

Where are you gonna get an ajumma perm when you're older?

When is your friend gonna meet you for lunch tomorrow?

Why are/aren't you gonna get a taxi home after drinking tomorrow night?

Or are you gonna stay out all night? When are you gonna call your Mom to tell her you're not coming home?

 Ask students to provide examples from their discussions using the 'useful vocabulary'.

✳ Add 3 more relevant and/or common errors from the students' discussion. Correct together on the board.

1. _____

2. _____

3. _____

✳ Please correct these sentences with a partner then check together as a class.

6. I'm gonna do straight home and sleep _____

7. Why are/aren't you gonna eat dog food at the start of next summer? _____

8. Are you gonna study hardly next class? _____

9. Are you gonna have a wedding plan in the next 10 years? _____

Take turns asking and answering the corrected questions with a partner.

Critical Thinking & Discussion

9. Disagreeing with someone and answering questions

There are a couple of important things to remember when you are disagreeing with someone in a discussion context. Sticking to them will ensure that the discussion continues to move smoothly and that unpleasant situations can be avoided.

The first of these things is to disagree politely. This can best be done by acknowledging the point or points that another person has made, and by staying calm and relaxed. It also goes without saying that if you maintain a respectful tone than the chances of someone listening and taking on what you have to say are much higher.

Secondly, you need to explain in full why you disagree with someone. If possible use facts and figures. Simply disagreeing with someone, without offering your reasons, is both impolite and unintellectual.

Disagreeing politely:

- I know what you mean, but...
- Yes, but don't you think...?
- I can see your point, but...
- Well, I don't think it's as simple as that.
- I partly agree, but...
- Well, I'm not so sure about that.
- Yeah, but the problem is that...
- Yeah, that's true, but on the other hand...
- You could be right but I think that...
- That's not entirely true.
- I'm sorry to disagree with you, but...
- don't think I completely agree.

Disagreeing more strongly:

- I totally disagree!
- You can't be serious!
- You must be joking/kidding!
- No way! That's crazy!

 Check off each of these statements after using them in today's discussion.

✳ Discuss/Debate these topics with your partner or group

- How are you going to improve all of your English skills?
- Are you going to travel overseas before getting a job? Why/Why not?

Review

What did we study today? Please provide three examples with correct responses. Say these correct sentences together as a class.

Preview

Please read through the materials for our next class together. Prepare any questions that you may have and we can discuss them in the warm-up session during the next class.

Have a great day. See you next class! Goodbye!

11 We're on vacation in 3 weeks

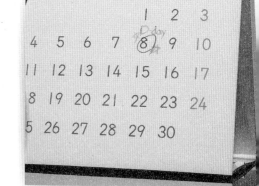

Previous Class Review

❋ What did we do in the previous lesson?
(Going to)
Elicit examples from students of:

* common questions
* natural responses
* relevant vocab

❋ Write these up on the board and practice them together.
What natural expressions did we work on in the previous class?
(Whaddaya gonna do?). Ask students for some key examples
(prompt/guide them if necessary). Put them on the board and
practice saying them correctly together.

 Practice these together with a partner for a few minutes.

Warm-Up

❋ When do we use the prepositions of time 'in, on, at, during, after, later, for, by, until, within'?
Brainstorm the relevant grammar and write in on the board.

* Prepositions of time: 'At' is used to show a specific time, 'on' is for a certain day, 'in' describes a period of time. 'During' is used before a noun of activity, 'after' means when an activity/action has ended, 'later' comes after a time expression that is not now, and 'for' shows an intention of action in a stated time period. 'By' means before a deadline, 'until' describes an action continuing to an end point, 'Within' means inside a limited time period. 'In' also comes before a time period and means 'from now'.

❋ Get some real-world, personalized examples for each one from students (to be written on the board).

1. _____   2. _____

3. _____   4. _____

5. _____ 6. _____

7. _____ 8. _____

9. _____ 10. _____

In (from now): _____

 Now students can open their textbooks and write correct examples from the board in the section above. Then take turns asking and answering these questions with a partner (ask more follow-up questions).

Language Focus

At	See you at 2pm tomorrow.
时间	明天两点见面。
On	I'm going back to Australia on Tuesday / on July 7 / on Independence Day.
星期/日期	星期二/7月7日/在独立纪念日我要准备回到澳大利亚
In	I'm gonna get a car in December / in 2024 / in Winter.
月/年/季节	在12月/2024年/冬天打算买个车。
During	During my vacation, I wanna break up with my girl/boyfriend.
期间	假期之间，我想跟女朋友/男朋友分手。
For	I'm gonna learn some Spanish for my trip in September.
	我将为我九月份的旅行学习一些西班牙语。
After	What's the first thing you're gonna buy after you get a job?
	在你找到工作之后，你想要买的第一个东西是什么？
Later	Last year I lost my phone in Itaewon, but I found it 2 days later.
	去年我在梨泰院丢了手机，但是两天后我找到了它。
By (before)	We have to get fit by the start of Summer!
	我们必须在夏天开始前恢复健康！
Until	I will study for 10 hours every day until our exams finish.
	我每天要学习10个小时，直到考试结束。
Within	If my brother doesn't get a job within the next month, my parents are gonna kill him.
	如果我弟弟下个月还找不到工作，我的父母就会杀了他。

 Take turns saying these examples to your partner and make some examples of your own for each one.

❋ Complete these sentences with a partner. Work together. (while speaking out loud)

1. Where are you gonna go _____ class?

2. I have to finish my assignment _____ 4pm _____ Monday.

3. I'm going to Seokcho (束草) next Thursday, but I'll come back 3 days _____ .

4. I'm really looking forward to going to Guam _____ 2 months. How long will you stay there? I'll stay there _____ 5 days.

5. I have a yoga class _____ 11am tomorrow and I will stay there _____ 2pm. _____ the class I will really do my best.

6. _____ August I'm going to China. I have to prepare my visa _____ the next 6 weeks.

🎓 Now practice these examples with your partner and make some more if you can.

Useful Vocabulary

❋ Try to use all of these words in your discussions today. Check them off as you use each one.

Drop by (顺便来访)	Wander around (徘徊)	My own apartment (我自己的公寓)
Play it by ear (见机行事)	Dream partner (梦想的伙伴)	Ancestral ceremony (祖先的仪式)
Free time (自由时间)	Positive attitude (积极的态度)	Innovative (革新的)
Efficiently (有效的)	One-way trip (单程旅行)	

Main Activity

✳ Practise asking and answering these questions using the correct grammar.

Ask more follow-up questions (Who/When/Where/Why/What/Which/How...?)

What are your immediate/short-term/long-term plans after you graduate?

You said you have another class at 5pm, but what are you up to later?

Do we have to prepare anything for the next class?

Where do you think you'll live in 10 years?

What do you think you'll be doing at 11pm this Friday night?

What do you usually do on Friday nights in Summer?

✳ Now, please also correct these sentences with a partner then check together as a class.

1. I will go to my hometown 2 weeks later _____

2. We should complete our homework until p.m. 6 in Friday, right?

_____

3. Are you gonna stay at your brother's house during 2 weeks?

_____

4. Do you have a flight to catch at Wednesday to 10pm _____

 Take turns asking and answering the corrected questions with a partner.

Natural English

✳ Practise the natural English expressions below.

I'm gonna meet my girl/boyfriend in Sinchon at 7pm on Saturday.
星期六晚上七点我会在新村见我的女朋友/男朋友。

I have a doctor's appointment next Thursday in Jongno.
下星期四我在钟路预约了医生。

I'm going on a date tonight with a girl/guy that I met the
other day.
我今晚要和一个我前几天见过的女孩/男孩约会。

I have a business meeting to go to this afternoon at 3.
今天下午三点我有一个商务会议要去。

Sorry, I can't make the workshop on Sunday because I
have a prior engagement. (Is it true?)
不好意思，我不能在周日开研讨会，因为我有约在先。(真的吗?)

My friends and I are having a get-together on Friday night. D'ya wanna come along?
我和我的朋友们星期五晚上要聚会。你想一起来吗?

More Yes/No questions… (Be sure to ask follow-up questions, also.)

What do you think are the most important things to learn during your time at university?

Do you have to prepare anything for Zhongqiu (中秋)?

What do you hope to achieve by the end of this year?

Ask students to provide examples from their
discussions using the 'useful vocabulary'.

You will enjoy your life until you get married! Do you agree or disagree?

Do you plan to get married within the next 8 years?

✳ Write 3 relevant and/or common errors from the students' discussion (on the board) to be corrected.

1. _____

2 _____

3. _____

✳ Now, please also correct these sentences with a partner then check together as a class.

5. Do you have a breakfast at the morning for the weekend? _____

6. Will you have a promise to play with your boy/girlfriend at 7pm on Friday?

_____

7. Do you have a schedule to meet your seniors or juniors in the Summer vacation?

_____

8. Would you like to marry with a talent after 5 years? _____

 Now ask the completed questions above to your partner and discuss.

Critical Thinking & Discussion

10. Summarizing the discussion

Evaluate what has been accomplished, assess what new learning people are taking home, and provide closure, e.g. through a summary of the main points, with the help of key terms or the day's agenda on the board, and by asking if there are questions, etc.

When giving a summary, we should cover all these points

- The problem in brief
- Majority point of view
- Dissenting viewpoints
- Whether the group has been able to reach a consensus or not

> Check off each of these points when giving a summary of today's discussion.

✳ Discuss/Debate these topics with your partner or group

- Do you think smoking should be allowed in public on Friday and Saturday night? When?
- Do you think children should have a curfew? What time should they be home by, and until what age?

Review

What did we study today? Please provide three examples with correct responses. Say these correct sentences together as a class.

Preview

Please read through the materials for our next class together. Prepare any questions that you may have and we can discuss them in the warm-up session during the next class.

Have a great day. See you next class!   BYE   BYE

12 Do you wanna hang out on the weekend?

Previous Class Review

✳ What did we do in units 7 to 11?
For each one, elicit examples
from students of:

- common questions
- natural responses
- relevant vocab

✳ Write these up on the board and practice them together.

 Practice these together with a partner for a few minutes.

Warm-Up

✳ When do we use 'phrasal verbs'? Elicit the relevant grammar and write in on the board.

- 'Phrasal verbs' are very common in natural, spoken English
- The structure is 'Verb + preposition' or 'verb + adverb + preposition'
- They are sometimes used to show emphasis or completion
- Much more often, they have a totally different meaning from the base verb

✳ Get some real-world, personalized examples from students (to be written on the board).

1. _____

2. _____

3. _____

 *Now students can open their textbooks and write correct examples from the board in the section above.
Then take turns asking and answering these questions with a partner (ask more follow-up questions).*

Language Focus

Verb + preposition	Who will look after our baby while we go drinking? 我们去喝酒的时候谁来照顾我们的孩子？
Verb + adverb + preposition	We need someone to take care of our kid immediately. 我们需要有人立即照顾我们的孩子。
Emphasis	When are you stressed out? Could you all please stand up / sit down? 你什么时候压力很大？你能站起来/坐下吗？
Completion	C'mon, drink up (eat up / finish off)! It's time to go. 来吧，喝完（吃完）！该走了。
Different meanings	Please put out (extinguish) your cigarette. You're not allowed to smoke here. 请熄掉你的烟。你不能在这里抽烟。

Let's put off (postpone) our tennis match until next weekend. It's raining.
我们把网球比赛推迟到下周末吧。下雨了。

I can't put up with (tolerate) people who chew gum loudly in class.
我无法忍受在课堂上大声嚼口香糖的人。

✽ Complete these sentences with a partner. Work together. (while speaking out loud)

1. When you're feeling _____, what do you do to cheer yourself _____?

2. Do you prefer to stand _____ in a crowd, or would you rather blend _____?

3. Who do you take _____ the most; your mom or your dad?

4. Do you think that capital punishment should be done away _____?

 Now ask these completed questions to your partner and discuss.

Cheer up & Smile !

Useful Vocabulary

❋ Try to use all of these words in your discussions today. Check them off as you use each one.

Awkward (笨拙的)   Luxurious (豪华的)   Reunion (重聚)   Fancy (设想)

Hooked on (着迷)   Stingy (吝啬的)   Essential (必要的)   Binge (drinking) (饮酒作乐)

Kick back (退还)   Get fit (健身)   Survive (幸存)   Pass out (分发)

Black out (中断)

Main Activity

❋ Practise speaking using these questions using the correct grammar.

Ask more follow-up questions (Who/When/Where/Why/What/Which/How…?)

Where is a great place to kick back on summer vacation?

Have you ever kept in touch with someone you've broken up with?

Do you usually have dinner at home or eat out?

How often do you get together with your high school friends?

Do you think more people exercise outdoors or work out at a gym?

❋ Add 3 relevant and/or common errors from the students' discussion. Correct together and leave the corrected sentences on the board.

1. _____

2. _____

3. _____

✳ Please correct these sentences with a partner then check together as a class.

1. You look stressed! How can you endure that? Cheer up!

_____

2. Come down! You can do it! Hang in there! Harden up!

_____

3. How often do you going out with your friends?

_____

4. What are some of your favorite places to hang up?

_____

5. Does Hye-soo have a wedding plan two years after with her talent lover?

_____

 Take turns asking and answering the corrected questions with a partner.

Natural Expressions/Pronunciation Practice

✳ Practise the natural English expressions and pronunciation of the highlighted words below.

There are those that wonder whether they would rather doze, breathe or breed in this weather.

See ya later! Yeah, take it easy! Thanks, you too.

After phoning your friendly wife on Friday, feel free to half or fully finish filling in four or five difficult profile forms in the office, if that's fine, Phillip.

Whaddaya gonna do after class?

Where are ya gonna meet your boy/girlfriend after your appointment at the medical clinic?

More Yes/No questions… (Be sure to ask follow-up questions, also.)

How hard do you think it is to give up smoking?

What are some things that you couldn't do without?

What are you really looking forward to doing in the future?

Do you know anyone who's blacked out or passed out from drinking too much?

How would you get by on W10,000 for a whole week?

Ask students to provide examples from their discussions using the 'useful vocabulary'.

✤ Write 3 more relevant and/or common errors from the students' discussion (on the board). Then correct them together.

1. _____

2. _____

3. _____

✤ Now, please also correct these sentences with a partner then check together as a class.

6. Have you ever fallen off with a friend or relative? _____

7. When you're worn up, what's a good pick-me-up? _____

8. What's a shocking surprise that you found away about a famous person?

_____

9. Do you want to go to shopping later? _____

Take turns asking and answering the corrected questions with a partner.

Presentation Topics

✳ Choose one of these topics and prepare a short presentation with a partner/partners.

- What are you really looking forward to doing in the next few years?

- Where was the best place you kicked back last year?

- Give an example of a time someone said, 'Hang in there!' to you.

- What are you going to achieve by the end of this year?

- What will you do during your vacation, starting in 2 weeks?

Review

What did we study today? Please provide three examples with correct responses. Say these correct sentences together as a class.

Preview

Please read through the materials for our next class together. Prepare any questions that you may have and we can discuss them in the warm-up session during the next class.

Goodbye & good luck

Have a great day. See you next class!

13 This is so exciting. I'm thrilled

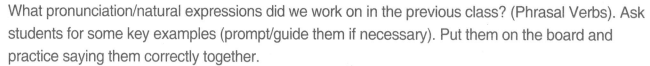

Previous Class Review

✳ What did we do in the previous lesson?
Elicit examples from students of:

* common questions
* natural responses
* relevant vocab

✳ Write these up on the board and
practice them together.
What pronunciation/natural expressions did we work on in the previous class? (Phrasal Verbs). Ask
students for some key examples (prompt/guide them if necessary). Put them on the board and
practice saying them correctly together.

 Practice these together with a partner for a few minutes.

Warm-Up

✳ When do we use '-ed or –ing adjectives'? Brainstorm the relevant grammar and write it on the board.

* '-ing adjectives' (It is/was exciting, boring, confusing) describe the characteristics of things and situations
(which cause emotions or feelings)
* '–ed adjectives' (I am/was excited, bored, confused) describe the reaction (emotion/feelings) felt by people
(or maybe animals)

✳ Get some real-world, personalized examples from students (to be written on the board).

1. _____

2. _____

3. _____

 Now students can open their textbooks and write correct examples from the board in the section above.
Then take turns asking and answering these questions with a partner (ask more follow-up questions).

Language Focus

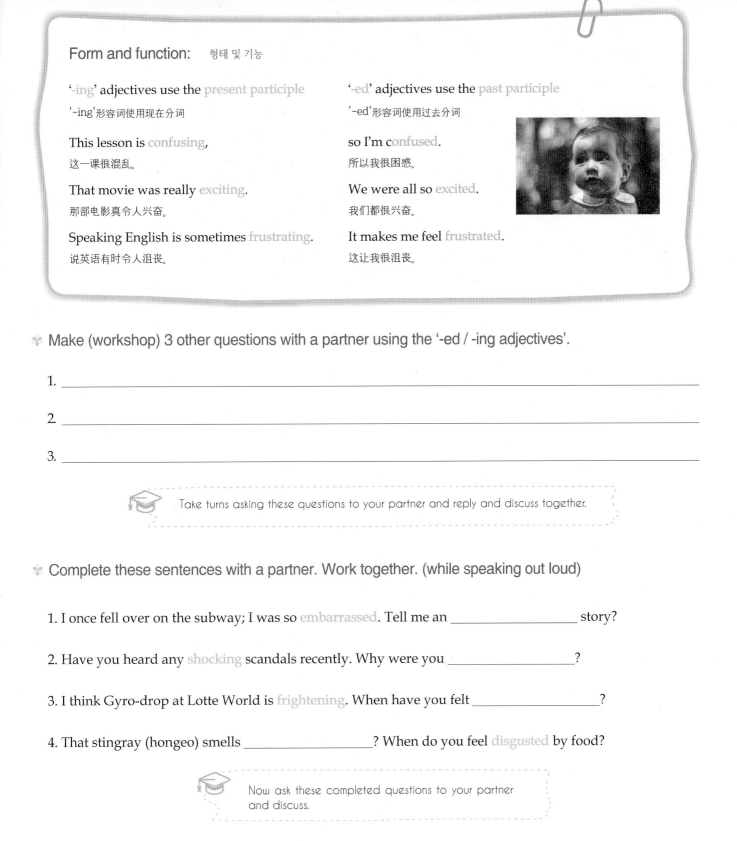

Form and function: 형태 및 기능

'-ing' adjectives use the present participle

'-ing'形容词使用现在分词

'-ed' adjectives use the past participle

'-ed'形容词使用过去分词

This lesson is confusing,

这一课很混乱。

so I'm confused.

所以我很困惑。

That movie was really exciting.

那部电影真令人兴奋。

We were all so excited.

我们都很兴奋。

Speaking English is sometimes frustrating.

说英语有时令人沮丧。

It makes me feel frustrated.

这让我很沮丧。

✳ Make (workshop) 3 other questions with a partner using the '-ed / -ing adjectives'.

1. _____

2. _____

3. _____

> 🎓 Take turns asking these questions to your partner and reply and discuss together.

✳ Complete these sentences with a partner. Work together. (while speaking out loud)

1. I once fell over on the subway; I was so embarrassed. Tell me an _____ story?

2. Have you heard any shocking scandals recently. Why were you _____?

3. I think Gyro-drop at Lotte World is frightening. When have you felt _____?

4. That stingray (hongeo) smells _____? When do you feel disgusted by food?

> 🎓 Now ask these completed questions to your partner and discuss.

Useful Vocabulary

✳ Try to use all of these words in your discussions today. Check them off as you use each one.

Informative (信息丰富的、有益的)   Stressful (有压力的)   Offensive (无礼的，冒犯的)

Off the market (退出市场，下架)   Staggering (惊人的、蹒跚的)

Main Activity

✳ Practise asking and answering these questions using the correct grammar.

Ask more follow-up questions (Who/When/Where/Why/What/Which/How…?)

When have you felt truly surprised?

What's the most interesting website that you check out?

Can you think of any politicians who are insulting?

Do you think studying or working is more tiring?

Would you be disappointed or pleased (happy) if your favourite celebrity got married?

✳ Add 3 relevant and/or common errors from the students' discussion. Correct together and leave the corrected sentences on the board.

1. _____

2. _____

3. _____

✳ Now, please also correct these sentences with a partner then check together as a class.

1. I'm really boring. I have nothing to do. You? _____

2. Do you satisfy your textbook? _____

3. When do you feel exhausting? _____

4. How do you think about Bollywood movies? _____

5. Music videos make me very entertaining? _____

 Take turns asking and answering the corrected questions with a partner.

Natural Expressions

❋ Finish the sentences below (adjective + preposition) then your partner should ask you as many Wh questions as possible about your statement.

I'm interested in…

I'm bored/afraid/proud/scared of…

I'm good/bad at…

I'm happy/worried/excited/nervous about…

I'm known/responsible/famous for…

I'm similar/allergic/addicted/opposed/kind/rude/engaged/married to…

I'm different from…

I'm pleased/satisfied/disappointed/annoyed/angry with…

I'm surprised by…

More Discussion Questions… (Be sure to ask follow-up questions, also.)

❋ Describe these things to your partner. Then take turns explaining how you would feel if you saw/did that.

A cockroach in your lunch / Korea winning the World Cup Football / Drinking a cool beer after playing sport

An ajumma pushing you out of the way to take the last seat on the subway / Farting during a job interview

Drinking hot chocolate on a freezing Winter's day / A mosquito flying around close to your ears all night

Watching Infinity challenge (무한도전) / Listening to your relatives tell you how to live your life

Losing your phone / Waking up in a strange place / Giving a speech in public and freezing on stage

Waiting over an hour to get a taxi home on a Friday night / Eating live octopus (sanakji)

Hanging out listening to music on a Sunday afternoon

✳ Make up some examples of your own and discuss the characteristics and reactions to these things, e.g.

'That sounds _____ing' / 'I'd be _____ed if I saw/did that'. Ask follow-up questions to your partner.

Ask students to provide examples from their discussions using the 'useful vocabulary'.

✳ Write 3 more relevant and/or common errors from the students' discussion (on the board). Then correct them together.

1. _____

2. _____

3. _____

✳ Now, please also correct these sentences with a partner then check together as a class.

6. He was so rude. I insulted _____

7. Hiking is very tired _____

8. That show is not interested to me _____

9. It's very irritate me _____

10. She makes me funny _____

11. I not satisfy with the dinner _____

12. Modern art is not fascinate _____

13. An international traveler asked me a question on the street and I couldn't speak English well, so I felt so confusing/shy/terrible _____

_____

Take turns saying the corrected statements with a partner.

Critical Thinking & Discussion

11. How to lead a discussion

Once the number of speakers in a group discussion reaches a certain number, a leader or facilitator becomes invaluable for ensuring an effective discussion. A good facilitator should:

- Create a safe and empowering atmosphere to get the best contribution from everyone.
- Give positive feedback for joining the discussion.
- Use encouraging body language and tone of voice, as well as words.
- Model the behavior and attitudes you want group members to employ.
- Be aware of people's reactions and feelings, and try to respond appropriately.
- Ask open-ended questions.
- Control your own biases.

 Check off each of these as you follow the suggestions for being a good facilitator in today's discussion

❋ Discuss/Debate these topics with your partner or group

- What experience in your life was truly fascinating?
- What do you think is really thrilling/annoying/satisfying/frustrating? Why?

Review

What did we study today? Please provide three examples with correct responses. Say these correct sentences together as a class.

Preview

Please read through the materials for our next class together. Prepare any questions that you may have and we can discuss them in the warm-up session during the next class.

Have a great day. See you next class! **Goodbye!**

14 What should I have for dinner?

Previous Class Review

✻ What did we do in the previous lesson?
(ed/ing adjectives)
Elicit examples from students of:

- common questions
- natural responses
- relevant vocab

✻ Write these up on the board and practice them together.
What natural expressions did we work on in the previous class? (adjective + preposition) Ask students for some key examples. Put them on the board and practice saying them correctly together.

 Practice these together with a partner for a few minutes.

Warm-Up

✻ How do we 'Give advice'? Brainstorm the relevant grammar and write it on the board.

- We can give soft advice using 'Why don't you?', 'You could always', and 'If I were you, I would…'
- 'Should', 'ought to', and 'had better' are examples of more regular advice.
- We can use 'have to', 'must', and 'need to' to show obligation and give very strong advice.

✻ Get some real-world, personalized examples from students (to be written on the board).

1. _____

2. _____

3. _____

 Now students can open their textbooks and write correct examples from the board in the section above. Then take turns asking and answering these questions with a partner (ask more follow-up questions).

Language Focus

(Suggestion)
)建议)

Why don't you try to eat buldak (火鸡)?
你为什么不试着吃火鸡呢？

You could always go to bed
earlier.
你可以早点睡觉。

If I were you, I'd (I would) ask
if I could borrow an umbrella.
如果我是你，我会问我是否可以借一
把伞。

(Advice)

(忠告)

You should go over and say,
'Hi!'.
你应该过去说"嗨!"

(Recommendation)
(推荐、建议)

You ought to stop drinking coffee in the evening.
你应该停止在晚上咖啡。

(Strong advice/Warning)
)强烈建议/警告)

You'd (You had) better hide that cigarette quickly.
你最好快点把香烟藏起来。

You'd better not be late for the train.
你最好不要错过火车。

(Obligation/Very strong advice)
(义务/非常强烈的建议)

He has to go to military service next year.
他明年要去服兵役。

You have to/must/need to watch the movie, 'Okja'. It's fantastic!
你一定要看《玉子》这部电影。它棒极了！

✽ Make (workshop) 3 other questions with a partner asking for advice.

1. _____

2. _____

3. _____

Take turns asking these questions to your partner and reply and discuss together.

❋ Complete these sentences with a partner. Work together. (while speaking out loud)

1. I know someone who sometimes drives after drinking. He'd _____ stop doing that. Any suggestions?

2. My partner sends so many Kakao Talk messages during class. If I _____ her, I'd…..

3. My brother's not very healthy, these days. What _____ he do?

4. You _____ to think seriously before changing your degree. Don't you think?

5. The taxi driver _____ (_____) stop at the red light. Do you always agree?

6. The bar is totally out of beer and soju (烧酒). Why _____ we try some…? / We _____ always try some…

 Now ask these completed questions to your partner and discuss.

Useful Vocabulary

❋ Try to use all of these words in your discussions today. Check them off as you use each one.

Internship (实习期)

Go cold turkey (突然戒掉原来上瘾的习惯)

Hair of the dog (解醉酒)

Insomniac (失眠症患者)

Tacky (俗气的)

Gathering (聚集、集会)

Matchmaking agency (婚介机构)

Lucrative (利润丰厚的)

Get in touch (保持联系)

Full of energy (精力充沛的)

Outgoing (外向的)

Main Activity

❋ Take turns giving advice to your partner in the following situations.

Try to use as many different ways as possible to give advice for each example.

I really wanna get a good job.

I have a terrible hangover.

I really want to find a girl/boyfriend as soon as possible.

I'm so bored. I have nothing to do tonight.

I seriously wanna be rich and famous.

I'm exhausted today, but I have another class and then I've gotta go to my part-time job later.

❋ Add 3 relevant and/or common errors from the students' discussion. Correct together and leave the corrected sentences on the board.

1. _____

2. _____

3. _____

❋ Now, please also correct these sentences with a partner then check together as a class.

1. I just threw up! I better to go to the hospital, right? _____

2. What kind of person I should marry? _____

3. Where's the most relaxing place to talk about with your friends? _____

4. Your dog stinks! Why don't wash him? _____

5. What must I to bring to the end-of-semester exam? _____

6. In my case, I was embarrassing when I give to presentation. You?

_____

Take turns asking and answering the corrected questions with a partner.

Pronunciation practice

✳ Practise the natural English pronunciation of the highlighted words below.

| Very – Berry | Van – Ban | Bet – Vet | Boat – Vote | Curb – Curve | Dub – Dove |

Our lovely wives drove to Venice in a van and arrived in November.

Victor, the very lively vet, lived in a valley above the village with his five doves.

More Discussion Questions: (Be sure to ask follow-up questions, also.)

Your best friend wants to get a tattoo of a dragon on her face. What advice would you give her?

My cousin is an outsider (wang-ta). How should he make friends?

I find it really hard to get to sleep. What should I do?

My dad really wants to meet some people from other countries. Any suggestions?

I'm desperate to give up smoking, but it's so hard. Any advice?

 Ask students to provide examples from their discussions using the 'useful vocabulary'.

✳ Write 3 more relevant and/or common errors from the students' discussion (on the board). Then correct them together.

1. _____

2. _____

3. _____

✳ Now, please also correct these sentences with a partner then check together as a class.

7. This dress isn't fit to me. Any tips? _____

8. I need get from Uijeongbu (议政府) to Gimpo airport (金浦机场) in 90 minutes. What the best way?

_____

9. How many helpful advices could you give to a Korean High School student?

_____

10. What should you say about Korean food which is not familiar with most of foreigner?

_____

11. How should I get to Mokpo (木浦)? Sorry, I don't know well.

 Take turns asking and answering the corrected questions with a partner.

Critical Thinking & Discussion

12. The finer points of discussion etiquette.

Do's:
- Respect what other speakers have to say and stay pleasant and courteous.
- Acknowledge when someone else makes a good point.
- Think before you speak!
- Speak clearly and confidently.
- Listen attentively to the ideas of others.
- Try and stay on topic, and try not to bring up unrelated or irrelevant information.
- Pay attention to your body language. Gestures like finger pointing or table thumping can appear very aggressive.
- Bring a pen and a notepad and take notes (or use your laptop).
- Introduce yourself before you speak if there is anyone taking part in the discussion that you do not know.

 Check off each of these forms of good etiquette after using them in today's discussion.

❋ Discuss/Debate these topics with your partner or group

- How should world governments work together to solve growing income inequality?
- In your opinion, should marijuana (大麻) be legalised (合法化) in Korea? Why/Why not?

Review

What did we study today? Please provide three examples with correct responses. Say these correct sentences together as a class.

Preview

Please read through the materials for our next class together. Prepare any questions that you may have and we can discuss them in the warm-up session during the next class.

Have a great day. See you next class!

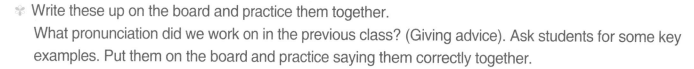

15 I am the greatest!

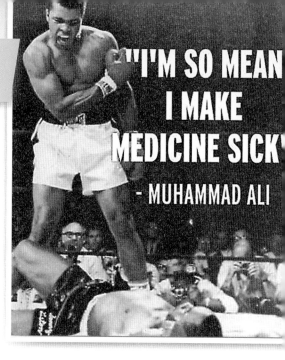

"I'M SO MEAN
I MAKE
MEDICINE SICK"
- MUHAMMAD ALI

Previous Class Review

✳ What did we do in the previous lesson? (Wish & hope)
Elicit examples from students of:

- making a sentence using wish
- using hope in a sentence
- relevant vocab / natural expressions

✳ Write these up on the board and practice them together.
What pronunciation did we work on in the previous class? (Giving advice). Ask students for some key examples. Put them on the board and practice saying them correctly together.

Warm-Up

✳ When do we use comparatives? Give an example. How about superlatives? Example?

- We use a comparative to compare 1 person, thing, action, or group with another one
- We use a superlative to compare 1 person, thing, or action with the whole group that it belongs to

✳ Students should provide some real-world, personalized examples.

1. _____

2. _____

3. _____

 Now students can open their textbooks and write correct examples from the board in the section above. Then take turns asking and answering these questions with a partner (ask more follow-up questions).

Language Focus

1 syllable (big)

一个音节时（大的）

2 syllables ending in 'y' (spicy)

以"y"结尾的两个音节时（辛辣的）

2 or more syllables

两个或更多音节时

Busan is bigger than Daegu.

釜山比大邱大。

Teokkbokki is spicier than kimchi.

炒年糕比泡菜辣。

Buldak is the spiciest dish in Korea.

火鸡（韩国的一种酱料鸡）是韩国最辣的食物。

Who is more handsome than G-Dragon?

谁比权志龙还帅？

Who's the most handsome man is Korea?

谁是韩国最帅的男人？

Is English more complicated than Korean?

英语比韩语更复杂吗？

What's the most complicated language in the world?

世界上最复杂的语言是什么？

Seoul is the biggest city in Korea.

首尔是韩国最大的城市。

✳ Make 3 other questions with a partner using comparatives and superlatives.

1. _____

2. _____

3. _____

 Ask these questions to your partner and give the correct response.

✤ Complete these sentences with a partner. Work together. (while speaking out loud)

1. What is the scariest move you have _____ seen?

2. Which is more _____, classical music or trot?

3. _____ is the sexiest person in the world?

4. Soju is _____ than beer, huh?

5. The most dangerous person in the world is _____.

 Now ask these completed questions to your partner and discuss.

Natural Expressions Practice

✤ Practise the natural English expressions below.

He's short

He's very/really short (I really like chicken)

He's so short

He's too short, so he can't play basketball well

He isn't tall enough to play basketball well

Our president is very/really/so _____. Do you agree? He/She isn't _____ enough, right?

I'm very/really/so _____, but I'm not _____ enough. What do you think?

Who do you think is very/really/so kind/beautiful/handsome/ interesting/smart/funny? Why?

Who do you think isn't kind/beautiful/handsome/interesting/smart/funny enough? Why?

Useful Vocabulary

❋ Try to use all of these words in your discussions today. Check them off as you use each one.

Hilarious (非常滑稽的)	Struggling (奋斗的)	Spectacular (壮观的、惊人的)
Repulsive (令人厌恶的)	Overwhelming (压倒性的)	Tearjerker (催人泪下的电影或戏剧)
Almost perfect (几乎完美的)	Not that much difference (没有太大的区别)	
Mind-numbing (头脑麻木的)	Feeble (微弱的)	Box (cask) wine (酒桶)
Charismatic (有魅力的)	Captivating (迷人的)	

Main Activity

❋ Practise speaking using these questions using the correct grammar (verb tense).

Ask more follow-up questions (Who/When/Where/Why/What/Which/How...?)

Faster, Higher, Stronger

Do you think galbi (排骨) is tastier than samgyeopsal (五花肉)?

Which is more disgusting; beondegi (蝉蛹) or gopchang (牛小肠)?

Is Tokyo or Beijing farther from here?

Do you think Seoraksan (雪岳山) or Baekdusan (白头山) is more beautiful?

Do you wanna be more attractive or smarter? (You can't choose both)

New York is more crowded than Seoul. Do you think this statement is true or false?

Do ya (you) think the Doosan Bears (斗山熊，韩国棒球队队名) are better than the Lotte Giants (乐天巨人，韩国棒球队队名)?

❋ Add 3 relevant and/or common errors from the students' discussion. Correct together and leave the corrected sentences on the board.

1. _____

2. _____

3. _____

✳ Now, please correct these sentences together with a partner and then check together as a class.

1. Do you think summer is more better than winter? _____

2. Is your brother crazy than your sister? _____

3. Don't you think Disneyland (迪士尼乐园) is exciting more than Wolmido (月尾岛)?

_____

4. Is Bill Gates (比尔盖茨) richer Lee, Kun-hee (李健熙)? _____

5. I like you too much, don't you think? _____

🎓 Take turns asking and answering the corrected questions with a partner.

You're the best… (Be sure to ask follow-up questions, also.)

What's the most boring subject you've ever studied?

Who do you think's the funniest comedian in Korea/the world?

What's the saddest movie you've ever seen?

Whaddya think is the best K-pop band?

What do you think is the world's most useful invention ever?

Which TV show do you think is the most interesting these days?

🎓 Ask students to provide examples from their discussions using the 'useful vocabulary'.

✳ Add 3 more relevant and/or common errors from the students' discussion. Correct together and leave the sentences on the board.

1. _____

2. _____

3. _____

✳ Please correct these sentences together.

6. Is Barcelona most amazing place you've even visited? _____

7. Who is the most craziest person you know? _____

8. Is Myeong-dong (明洞) is the busier place in Seoul? _____

9. Hallasan (汉拿山) is the most high mountain in Korea, right? _____

10. Who's best hobby is hunting much Korean woman? _____

🎓 Now take turns asking and answering the corrected questions with a partner.

Critical Thinking & Discussion

13. The finer points of discussion etiquette.

Don'ts:

- Never insult, humiliate or ridicule another speaker.
- Don't be offended when someone disagrees with you.
- Don't interrupt or talk over other speakers.
- Pay attention to your tone of voice, and try not to ever sound angry or aggressive.
- Do not try to dominate your co-participants and give others plenty of opportunities to speak.

 Check off each of these styles of bad etiquette when you avoid using them in today's discussion.

❋ Discuss/Debate these topics with your partner or group

- Who has been the most influential person in Korean history/politics/sports/entertainment?
- Do you think books or TV have been more important in informing you about the world? In what ways? Give examples

Review

What did we study today? Please provide three examples with correct responses. Say these correct sentences together as a class.

Preview

Please read through the materials for our next class together. Prepare any questions that you may have and we can discuss them in the warm-up session during the next class.

Have a great day. See you next class!

Previous Class Review

❋ What did we do in the previous lesson?
(Comparatives & superlatives) What was/were the:

- target language
- key questions and responses
- relevant vocab
- natural expressions

❋ Write these up on the board and practice them together.
What natural expressions did we work on in the previous
class? (Do ya wanna…?). Ask students for some key
examples (prompt/guide them if necessary). Put them on the
board and practice saying them correctly together.

Warm-Up

❋ What is the Present Perfect? Explain the relevant grammar. When is it used?

- Have/has + p.p. (past participle)
- Used to talk about events that you have experienced in the past that are still relevant now

❋ Students should provide some real-world, personalized examples.

1. _____

2. _____

3. _____

 Now students can open their textbooks and write correct examples from the board in the section above.
Then take turns asking and answering these questions with a partner (ask more follow-up questions).

Language Focus

I have been to Jeju Island.
我去过济州岛。

I've never been to Jeju Island.
我从来没去过济州岛。

Have you (ever) been to Jeju Island?
你(曾经)去过济州岛吗？

Yes, I have. / No, I haven't been there, yet.
是的，我去过。/不，我还没有去过那里。

Has _____ been to Jeju Island?
_____去过济州岛吗？

Yes, she has. /No, she hasn't.
是的，她去过。/不，她没去过。

Where have you been/visited?
你去过/拜访过哪里？

I've been to/visited _____.
我去过/拜访过_____。

I've lived in Korea for 9 months / since last year, but I haven't been to Jeju Island, yet.
我在韩国生活了9个月/从去年开始我住在韩国，但是我还没有去过济州岛。

I've already seen the new movie, 'Avengers 27'. How about you?
我已经看过新电影《复仇者联盟27》了。你呢？

Yeah, I've just seen it (I just saw it yesterday).
是的，我刚看(我昨天刚看的)。

❋ Make 3 other questions with a partner using the Present Perfect.

1. _____

2. _____

3. _____

🎓 Ask these questions to your partner and give the correct response.

Useful Vocabulary

❋ Try to use all of these words in your discussions today. Check them off as you use each one.

Bloated (发胀的)	Jet lag (时差)	Begging (乞讨)	Hard to catch (爱情观；很难赶上)
Laptop computer (笔记本电脑)	Secret admirer (暗恋者)		Stage fright (怯场)
Inspiring (振奋人心的)	Invigorating (精力充沛的)		Passionate (热情的)

✳ Complete these sentences with a partner. Work together. (while speaking out loud)

1. Have you _____ sung an English song at a singing room?

2. I have _____ the movie, 'About Time'. How about you?

3. How many times have you _____ soju?

4. Have you _____ late for this class? Why/Why not?

5. What is the strangest food that you have ever _____?

6. _____ you ever seen a K-pop star in real life? Who was it? Where?

 Now ask these completed questions to your partner and discuss.

Main Activity

✳ Practise speaking using these questions using the correct grammar. (verb tense)

Ask more follow-up questions (Who/When/Where/Why/What/Which/How…?)

Have you ever…

(eat) so much kalbi (ribs) that you felt sick? Where were you?

(speak) to a stranger in English? What did you say?

(fly) in a plane? How many times?

(give) money to a homeless person? When? How often?

(watch) a TV show/movie in English without Chinese subtitles?
Which show/movie was it? How much could you understand?

English for Chinese Speakers

✳ Add 3 relevant and/or common errors from the students' discussion. Correct together and leave the corrected sentences on the board.

1. _____

2. _____

3. _____

✳ Now, please also correct these sentences with a partner then check together as a class.

1. Have you ever ride on a roller-coaster? _____

2. Yes, I've ever ridden on a roller-coaster. You? _____

3. No, I did never have ride on a roller-coaster _____

4. Last year, I have been to Everland (爱宝乐园) _____

Ask the completed questions to your partner and discuss.

Natural Expressions Practice

✳ Practise the natural English expressions below.

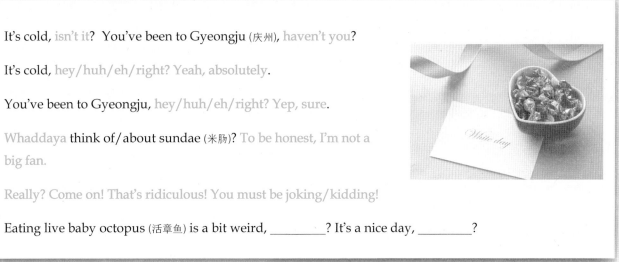

It's cold, isn't it? You've been to Gyeongju (庆州), haven't you?

It's cold, hey/huh/eh/right? Yeah, absolutely.

You've been to Gyeongju, hey/huh/eh/right? Yep, sure.

Whaddaya think of/about sundae (米肠)? To be honest, I'm not a big fan.

Really? Come on! That's ridiculous! You must be joking/kidding!

Eating live baby octopus (活章鱼) is a bit weird, _____? It's a nice day, _____?

Have you ever… (Be sure to ask follow-up questions, also.)

(buy) something expensive? What was it?

(receive) something on Valentine's Day/White Day? From
         whom?

(sleep) outside under the stars? Where were you?

(climb) to the top of Seorak Mountain (雪岳山)? How was
        the weather on that day?

(shout) at someone in public? Why?

 Ask students to provide examples from their discussions
using the 'useful vocabulary'.

✴ Add 3 more relevant and/or common errors from the students' discussion. Correct together and leave
   the sentences on the board.

1. _____

2. _____

3. _____

✴ Please correct these sentences with a partner then check together as a class.

5. I have been to Brazil where I have met many interesting people. You?

   _____

6. I have ever eaten frog's legs. Is it true? _____

7. Have you seen the news yesterday? _____

8. Had you ever been go Australia? _____

 Now take turns asking and answering the corrected
questions with your partner.

Critical Thinking & Discussion

14. Politely interrupting

- Can I just say something here?
- Can I stop you there for a moment?
- Can I just mention something?
- Can I just add something here?
- Before you move on, I'd like to say something.
- Excuse me for interrupting but…
- Excuse me for butting in but…
- Sorry for interrupting but….
- Just a moment, I'd like to….
- If I could just come in here. I think….

 Check off each of these ways to politely interrupt when you use them in today's discussion.

※ **Discuss/Debate these topics with your partner or group**

- What has changed in Korea over the last 15 years (culturally/politically/economically/socially)?
- Where have you been (and/or who have you met) that has given you knowledge about different cultures?

Review

What did we study today? Please provide three examples with correct responses. Say these correct sentences together as a class.

Preview

Please read through the materials for our next class together. Prepare any questions that you may have and we can discuss them in the warm-up session during the next class.

Have a great day. See you next class!

THANK YOU AND SEE YOU LATER

17 | What were you thinking?

Previous Class Review

✤ What did we do in the previous lesson?
(Present perfect)
Elicit examples from students of:

- common questions
- natural responses
- relevant vocab

✤ Write these up on the board and practice them together.
What natural expressions did we work on in the previous
class? (Tag questions). Ask students for some key
examples (prompt/guide them if necessary). Put them on
the board and practice saying them correctly together.

 Practice these together with a partner for a few minutes.

Warm-Up

✤ When do we use the 'past continuous'? Brainstorm the relevant grammar and write it on the board.

- The 'past continuous' is used to talk about something that was happening in the past:
  - before and after a particular time or action
  - continuing for some time / again and again / showing change or growth

✤ Get some real-world, personalized examples from students (to be written on the board).

1. _____

2. _____

3. _____

 Now students can open their textbooks and write correct examples from the board in the section above.
Then take turns asking and answering these questions with a partner (ask more follow-up questions).

Language Focus

Form and function: 形式和功能

(In the past) (过去)	Past tense of *be* with the *-ing* form of the verb be动词的过去时态+V-ing
(before and after a particular time) (在一个特定的时间之前和之后)	I was drinking dong dong ju at 4am last Sunday morning. 上周日早上四点我正在喝米酒。
(before and after a particular action) (在特定的动作之前和之后)	She was eating teokbokki when she spilled it on my shirt. 她在吃炒年糕时溅到了我的衬衫上。

(continuing for some time) (持续一段时间)	(again and again) (一次又一次)	(showing change or growth) (显示变化或增长)
Everyone was cheering. 每个人都在欢呼。	They were arguing every day. 他们天天吵架。	Korea was modernising rapidly. 韩国正在迅速实现现代化。

✳ Make (workshop) 3 other questions with a partner using the 'past continuous'.

1. _____

2. _____

3. _____

> 🎓 Take turns asking these questions to your partner and reply and discuss together.

✳ Complete these sentences with a partner. Work together. (while speaking out loud)

1. While I _____ playing on my computer last night, the internet dropped out. How do you think I felt?

2. I was _____ almost around the clock when I was a High School student. Do you think that's healthy?

3. My friend was always _____ overtime at his last company. Is that common?

4. They _____ practising piano every day when they were young? Was that useful?

> 🎓 Now ask these completed questions to your partner and discuss.

Useful Vocabulary

❋ Try to use all of these words in your discussions today. Check them off as you use each one.

Daydreaming (白日梦)	Irritate (刺激)	Siblings (兄弟姐妹)
Mother-in-law (婆婆，岳母)	Heat wave (热浪)	Passionate (热情的)
Obsessed (痴迷的，着迷的)	Road rage (路怒症)	Hangover (宿醉)
Gossiping (闲聊)	Bother (麻烦，烦扰)	Affluent (富裕的)

Main Activity

❋ Practise asking and answering these questions using the correct grammar.

Ask more follow-up questions (Who/When/Where/Why/What/Which/How…?)

Sorry, I wasn't paying attention. What are we supposed to do?

What were you doing at 10pm last Friday night?

Has anyone ever told you to stop when you were whistling at night?

Who were you always spending time with when you were young?

Were you happy to be interrupted when you were studying recently?

Where were you going when I saw you yesterday afternoon?

What were you thinking about just before this class started?

Which band/group were you listening to over and over again last year?

Have you ever forgotten to eat or drink when you were playing computer games? For how long?

Were you studying at 9pm last night?

✳ Add 3 relevant and/or common errors from the students' discussion. Correct together and leave the corrected sentences on the board.

1. _____

2. _____

3. _____

✳ Now, please also correct these sentences with a partner then check together as a class.

1. Do you play with your phone, while you was waiting for this class to start?

_____

2. Have you ever hurted yourself, while you snowboarding/water-skiing etc?

_____

3. Did you get any pop-up ads while you were were playing with your computer recently?

_____

4. Have you ever falling asleep, when you was sitting in a class?

_____

 Take turns asking and answering the corrected questions with a partner.

Pronunciation practice

✳ Practise the natural English pronunciation of the highlighted words below.

| Sue – Zoo | Sip – Zip | Bus – Buzz | Price – Prize | Sap – Zap | Niece – Knees |
| Face – Phase | Ice – Eyes | Sink – Zinc | Race – Raise | Pace - Pays | C – Z OL - link |

Susan and Liz went to the amazing zoo with Mrs. Jones to see zebras and lions.

Isn't the noise of the buzzing bees more surprising than those guys say it was?

What questions have you learnt in these languages in recent years: Chinese, Vietnamese, Japanese?

More Discussion Questions… (Be sure to ask follow-up questions, also.)

Have you ever been bothered by someone, while you were taking a test/exam?

Did it ever pour down (rain very heavily) while you were playing sport/ having a picnic etc?

Have you ever seen someone shout out the window while they were driving?

Did your alarm go off this morning while you were still sleeping?

How was Korea changing during the 1960s compared to these days?

Between what ages were you practising a musical instrument every day?

What were you doing while your Mom was making dinner last night? Why weren't you helping?

When's the last time your head was aching all day?

 Ask students to provide examples from their discussions using the 'useful vocabulary'.

✴ Write 3 more relevant and/or common errors from the students' discussion (on the board). Then correct them together.

1. _____

2. _____

3. _____

✴ Now, please also correct these sentences with a partner then check together as a class.

5. When did you last shout while you were listened to music using earphones?

_____

6. Did you check out your phone while you are talking to someone recently?

_____

7. When's the last time you fell asleep while you were travelling on the subway?

_____

8. He said me he wasn't feeling well? _____

9. As for me, I was dancing on p.m. 11 last night. You? _____

 Take turns asking and answering the corrected questions with your partner.

Critical Thinking & Discussion

15. Keeping the discussion on track

- Let's come back to that.
- I want to hear more about that afterwards.
- Let's come back to that in a minute.
- Let me just finish what I was saying…
- We're definitely going to talk about that next.
- Sure thing. I want to talk about that too.
- I want to hear more. But before I lose my train of thought…
- As I was saying,…
- Getting back to what I was saying…
- Where was I? (*say this if you need some help remembering what you were saying!*)
- Continuing where I left off, …
- As I was explaining,…

 Check off each of these expressions when you use them in today's discussion.

✲ Discuss/Debate these topics with your partner or group

- What are the most important things that you were learning every day before starting school?
- What was happening every day regularly during the Joseon Dynasty (朝鮮王朝), that doesn't happen often these days?

Review

What did we study today? Please provide three examples with correct responses. Say these correct sentences together as a class.

Preview

Please read through the materials for our next class together. Prepare any questions that you may have and we can discuss them in the warm-up session during the next class.

Have a great day. See you next class!

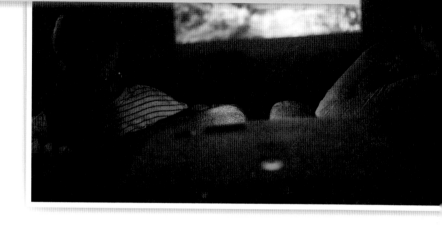

18 | Were you checking out the amazing movie?

Previous Class Review

✳ What did we do in the lessons 13-17?
Elicit examples from students of:

- common questions
- natural responses
- relevant vocab

✳ Write these up on the board and practice them together.
What pronunciation/natural expressions did we work on in the previous 5 classes? Ask students for some key examples (prompt/guide them if necessary). Put them on the board and practice saying them correctly together.

 Practice these together with a partner for a few minutes.

Warm-Up

✳ When are some different genres of movies? What kinds are your favorite? Name some specific movies that you like from each genre.
Get some examples from students (to be written on the board).

1. _____

2. _____

3. _____

 Now is an appropriate time for students to open their textbooks and write down their 3 favorite genres and at least one movie for each one in the section above.

Language Focus

Tell me about the movie:

What genre is it?	Action, comedy, horror, animation, Sci-Fi (SF) etc
What's the plot?	Explain the story
When was it made?	Recently, last year, 5 years ago, in 1997 etc
Where/When was it set?	What's the location and time period of the story etc
Who are the main characters?	Describe the main people in the movie
Who's the star/main actor?	Song Kang-ho, Meryl Streep, Tom Cruise etc
Who are the supporting actors?	Emma Stone, Bradley Cooper, Bae Doona, etc
Would you recommend this movie?	Why/Why not?

Using the 3 movies you named before, ask and answer the previous questions with your partner.

* Add 3 relevant and/or common errors from the students' discussion. Correct together and leave the corrected sentences on the board.

1. _____

2. _____

3. _____

* Complete these sentences with a partner. Work together. (while speaking out loud)

1. Do you think predictable or innovative movies are _____ interesting?

2. What movie would you tell your friends that they'd _____ see?

3. What's the _____ confusing movie you've ever seen?

4. We _____ watching a movie when I dropped my phone into my popcorn. Have you ever done that?

Now ask these completed questions to your partner and discuss.

Useful Vocabulary

❋ Try to use all of these words in your discussions today. Check them off as you use each one.

A babe (一个宝贝)   Stunning (令人震惊的)   Far-fetched (牵强的)

Slapstick comedy (闹剧)   Chick flick (针对女性的言情片)   Clumsy (笨拙的)

Moving (感动的)   Entertaining (令人愉快的)   Millennial (千年一次的)

Night owl (夜猫子)   Hysterical (歇斯底里的)

Main Activity

❋ Practise asking and answering these questions using the correct grammar.

Ask more follow-up questions (Who/When/Where/Why/What/Which/How…?)

Have you ever fallen over when you were going into/out of a movie theatre/theater?

Did your parents bother you last night, while you were trying to watch a movie at home?

What's the least impressive movie you've ever seen?

Have you ever seen a movie on DVD (VHS)? When was the last time?

What movie do you think is overrated/underrated?

❋ Add 3 relevant and/or common errors from the students' discussion. Correct together and leave the corrected sentences on the board.

1. _____

2. _____

3. _____

❋ Now, please also correct these sentences with a partner then check together as a class.

1. Do you feel irritated when you took off a bus at the wrong stop?

_____

2. In my think, you ought take KTX. Do you agree? _____

3. Is Park, Geun Hye (朴槿惠) smarter than she's father? _____

4. Have you ever tripped to Europe? _____

5. Were you eating kitchen in your chicken last night? _____

6. I'm best hobby is listen music and play computer game. You?

_____

7. Have you ever eaten 4 bottles of soju (烧酒。)? _____

 Take turns asking and answering the corrected questions with a partner.

Natural Expressions/Pronunciation Practice

✳ Practise the natural English expressions and natural English pronunciation of the highlighted words below.

What are you interested in/afraid of/good at/worried about/addicted to/satisfied with/surprised by?

Five vast vessels of vodka are more valuable than vitamins, vegetables & vaccines during your vacation

Who do you think is very/really/so funny? What is too difficult? Who isn't talented enough to be on TV?

Lovely day, hey?   Great movie, huh?   So hot, eh?   That's amazing, right?

Do you recognise that the size of the guy's eyes exists as a wise disguise winning a prize for spies?

More Discussion Questions… (Be sure to ask follow-up questions, also.)

In which movie do you think the main characters (actors) have the greatest chemistry?

Who do you think is the best looking actor/actress these days?

Do you think musicals are usually better than animation?

What's the most incredible martial arts movie you've ever seen?

What do you think is the funniest movie you've ever seen?

Ask students to provide examples from their discussions using the 'useful vocabulary'.

✻ Write 3 more relevant and/or common errors from the students' discussion (on the board). Then correct them together.

1. _____

2. _____

3. _____

✻ Now, please also correct these sentences with a partner then check together as a class.

8. Have you been one of staffs at company? _____

9. Why don't you exercise English every day? _____

10. Were you exciting to know that Ji-ae is was single? _____

11. I was really expecting this class? You? _____

12. Where's the most interesting place to go in Seoul for eye shopping?

_____

13. How do I do if I loose my bag on the subway? _____

14. We should wrap this up now. Are you ok? _____

🎓 Take turns asking and answering the corrected questions with your partner.

Presentation Topics

✻ Choose one of these topics and prepare a short presentation with a partner/partners.

- When have you felt the most exhausted/confused/ surprised/excited in your life?

- Do you think alcohol should be illegal? Why/Why not?

- What do you think is the best kind of music?

- Have you ever been to MT (on a team-building (bonding) activity/weekend)?

- How were people communicating before the internet and cell (mobile) phones?

Writing Test (optional):

Write 10 to 15 sentences about one of the topics above.

Presentation

Read carefully through your writing activity after you have checked the grammar with your teacher. Give a short presentation (1 to 2 minutes) about this to your partner or classmates. Ask if there are any questions and discuss further.

Review

What did we study today? Please provide three examples with correct responses. Say these correct sentences together as a class.

Preview

Please read through the materials for our next class together. Prepare any questions that you may have and we can discuss them in the warm-up session during the next class.

Bye-Bye

Have a great day. See you next class!

Previous Class Review

✤ What did we do in the previous lesson?
  Elicit examples from students of:

  • common questions
  • natural responses
  • relevant vocab

✤ Write these up on the board and practice them together.
  What pronunciation/natural expressions did we work on
  in the previous class? Ask students for some key examples
  (prompt/guide them if necessary). Put them on the board and practice saying them correctly together.

 Practice these together with a partner for a few minutes.

Warm-Up

✤ When do we use 'If conditionals'? Brainstorm the relevant grammar and write it on the board.

  • 'If conditionals' are used to describe things that:
    - 1st conditional (If + present + present) – are undisputed facts
    - 2nd conditional (If + present + will / might / can) – are likely or certain to happen in the future
    - 3rd conditional (If + past + would / might / could) – are possible, but very unlikely to happen
                                                          are unreal compared to the present situation

✤ Get some real-world, personalized examples from students (to be written on the board).

1. _____

2. _____

3. _____

 Now students can open their textbooks and write correct examples from the board in the section above.
Then take turns asking and answering these questions with a partner (ask more follow-up questions).

Language Focus

1st conditional (If + present + present) – are undisputed facts:

第一条件（如果+现在+现在）- 是无可争议的事实：

If it is summer in Seoul, it is winter in Sydney. / If you mix soju and beer, you get somaek.

如果首尔是夏天，悉尼就是冬天。 / 把烧酒和啤酒混在一起就成了炮弹酒。

2nd conditional (If + present + will / might / can) – are likely or certain to happen in the future:

第二个条件（如果+现在+将要/可能/可能）- 未来可能或肯定会发生：

If Ji hye gets the promotion, she will buy me dinner.

吉惠如果晋升的话，她将给我买晚餐。

If it doesn't stop raining, our BBQ might be cancelled.

如果雨不停的话我们的烤肉可能会被取消。

3rd conditional (If + past + would / might / could) – are possible, but very unlikely to happen:

第三个条件（如果+过去+将会/可能/可能）- 是可能的，但不太可能发生：

If I met my favorite movie star, I would scream uncontrollably.

如果我遇到我最喜欢的电影明星我会不由自主的尖叫。

- are unreal compared to the present situation:
- 与目前情况相比是不真实的：

If today were Sunday, I would stay in bed all day.

如果今天是星期天，我会整天躺在床上。

❋ Make (workshop) 3 other questions with a partner using conditionals.

1. _____

2. _____

3. _____

 Take turns asking and answering the corrected questions with a partner.

❋ Complete these sentences with a partner. Work together (while speaking out loud).

1. If I _____ my homework early, I'll go out tonight? You?

2. If you _____ vodka till 3am, you feel terrible the next day, right?

3. Where would you live, if you _____ live anywhere in the world?

4. If your apartment was on fire, what are the first 3 things you _____ save?

> 🎓 Now ask these completed questions to your partner and discuss.

Useful Vocabulary

❈ Try to use all of these words in your discussions today. Check them off as you use each one.

Rip-off (诈骗，偷窃)	Indecisive (犹豫不决的)	Gorgeous (华丽的)
Skip class (翘课)	Gullible (易受骗的)	Open-minded (开放的)
Skeptical (怀疑的)	Satisfying (满意的)	Get some R & R (rest and relaxation) (休息一下，放松一下)
Integrity and compassion (诚信和同情)		Tough choice (艰难的选择)

Main Activity

❈ Practise asking and answering these questions using the correct grammar.

Ask more follow-up questions (Who/When/Where/Why/What/Which/How…?)

If…?

If we don't have a class tomorrow, we can all relax. Good idea?

If Manchester United loses, I'll be really happy. How about you?

How would you feel if the price of cigarettes went up to 10,000 Won for a pack?

If you could choose anyone to be the next President of Korea/the US, who would you choose?

What would you choose if you could have either free English lessons or free chocolate for a year?

✽ Add 3 relevant and/or common errors from the students' discussion. Correct together and leave the corrected sentences on the board.

1. _____

2. _____

3. _____

✽ Now, please also correct these sentences with a partner then check together as a class.

1. If my age is 24, how many years before you think I should get a job/married?

   _____

2. If I said, 'Konnichiwa (日语你好的意思)!'. Are you understand?

   _____

3. If you lived near your school/office, it would be very comfortable, eh?

   _____

4. If you eat a medicine every day, will you be health? _____

Take turns asking and answering the corrected questions with your partner.

Natural Expressions

✽ Finish the sentences below (verb + preposition) then your partner should ask you as many Wh questions as possible about your statement.

I will wait/apologize/apply/ask/care/prepare/pay for...   I believe/specialize/succeed in...

He approved/died/smelled of...

They will suffer/recover/borrow/protect (you)/save (you) from...

I concentrated/relied/depended on...   I sometimes talk/worry about...

I belong/respond/refer/listen/introduce (someone)/explain (something) to...   I agree with...

More Discussion Questions: (Be sure to ask follow-up questions, also.)

If you could go out with a celebrity, who would you choose? Why?

If it snows a lot overnight, will you stay at home tomorrow?

If you could be any animal, what would you choose to be?

If you dream about pigs, you will be lucky with money soon?
Do you believe that?

If someone offered you $1,000,000 to take special pictures of
you and put them on the Internet, would you do it?

 Ask students to provide examples from their discussions
using the 'useful vocabulary'.

✳ Write 3 more relevant and/or common errors from the students' discussion (on the board). Then
correct them together.

1. _____

2. _____

3. _____

✳ Now, please also correct these sentences with a partner.

5. If shops have guests and hotels have customers, will the owners be happy?

_____

6. If you could choice to have any job, what would it be? _____

7. If you have a soccer mania, what should you do? _____

8. How would you feel if you met many of foreigners at the same time alone?

_____

 Take turns asking and answering the corrected questions
with your partner.

Critical Thinking & Discussion

16. Making sure everyone is involved in the discussion

- We'd be interested in what you all think.
- I've noticed that some of you have not said much. I hope we hear from you at some point.
- Please feel free to jump in at any point.
- Sang Hoon, you made some good points; let's hear from someone else.

▶ People monopolize the discussion.
- Say, 'I'd like to hear what the rest of the group has to say.'
- Ask another person a question just as soon as they pause.
- Ask for agreement or disagreement from others.
- Explain that you appreciate their comments, but it is important for everyone to have a chance to talk.
- Establish ground rules at the beginning (or mid-discussion) that one of the goals is to provide everyone an opportunity to share.

▶ Someone keeps changing the subject or goes on tangents.
- Say, 'That is very interesting but how do you feel about ...?'
- Refocus attention by saying "I know you are enjoying sharing your experience with each other, but there are some issues I would like to share with you now."
- Say, 'In order to accomplish our goal today, we really need to move on. Perhaps we can go back to this topic later.'

▶ People keep interrupting.
- 'Could we remember just to have one person talk at a time and let people finish their statements.'
- 'Okay..first Song Hee (宋熙), then Jun Seok (俊锡), then Seung Min 9(胜敏).'
- 'Sun Ok, you have got a lot of good points, but it is important to let Ho Jung finish, and then I know that Young Ah is dying to say something as well.'

 Check off each of these expressions when you use them in today's discussion.

✳ Discuss/Debate these topics with your partner or group
- How would your life have been different if you had been born a girl/ boy?
- If you were given 3 magic wishes, what would you wish for? Why?

Review

What did we study today? Please provide three examples with correct responses. Say these correct sentences together as a class.

Preview

Please read through the materials for our next class together. Prepare any questions that you may have and we can discuss them in the warm-up session during the next class.

Have a great day. See you next class!

20 | Do you like to go drinking?

Previous Class Review

❋ What did we do in the previous lesson?
   (If...) Elicit examples from students of:

   • common questions
   • natural responses
   • relevant vocab

❋ Write these up on the board and practice them together.
   What pronunciation/natural expressions did we work on in
   the previous class? (If…). Ask students for some key
   examples (prompt/guide them if necessary). Put them on the
   board and practice saying them correctly together.

 Practice these together with a partner for a few minutes.

Warm-Up

❋ When do we use 'infinitives and/or gerunds'? Brainstorm the relevant grammar and write in on the board.

   • Infinitive: verb followed by 'to + verb' – I want to eat pizza now
   • Gerund: verb followed by 'verb-ing' (gerund) – I enjoy cooking
   • The meaning is often similar between infinitives and gerunds and some verbs use both forms interchangeably
   • If there is a slight difference, it is that the 'infinitive' often refers to more specific actions (I plan to walk),
     whereas the 'gerund' often describes general activities - acting as a noun (I dislike walking).

❋ Get some real-world, personalized examples from students (to be written on the board).

1. _____

2. _____

3. _____

 Now students can open their textbooks and write correct examples from the board in the section above.
Then take turns asking and answering these questions with a partner (ask more follow-up questions).

Language Focus

Infinitive: verb followed by 'to + verb'　　不定式：动词后跟'to +动词'

　I need to tell you something urgently.　　我有急事要告诉你。

　I've decided to leave Korea for good.　　我决定永远离开韩国。

　I hope to meet you again sometime.　　我希望以后能再见到你。

　They're planning to eat a lot tonight.　　他们打算今晚吃很多东西。

　I can't afford to join you.　　我不能加入你。

Gerund: verb followed by 'verb-ing'　　动名词：动词后跟动词-ing

　He keeps telling us to talk more.　　他让我们继续说下去。

　I can't help falling in love with you.　　我情不自禁的爱上了你。

　That guy should give up smoking.　　那家伙应该戒烟。

　You should consider traveling more often.　你应该考虑经常旅游。

 Can you think of some more examples together?

Verbs followed by both infinitive - 'to + verb' & gerund: 'verb-ing'　　动词后跟不定式- to +动词&动名词：'动词-ing'

　I like to iron./ I like ironing.　　I will continue to play the piano./ I will continue playing the piano.

　我喜欢熨烫。　　　　　　　　　　我将会继续弹钢琴。

　My cousin loves to sing. / My cousin loves singing.　　I prefer to sleep. / I prefer sleeping.

　我表弟喜欢唱歌。　　　　　　　　　　　　　　　　　我更喜欢睡觉。

There are activities that use a combination infinitive & gerund (as a noun) forms, as in 'to go verb-ing':
有一些活动使用不定式和动名词的组合形式，如"to go verb-ing"：

　I want/like: to go hiking / to go swimming / to go bowling / to go fishing / to go skiing etc
　我想/喜欢:去徒步旅行/去游泳/去打保龄球/去钓鱼/去滑雪等

✳ Make (workshop) 3 other questions with a partner using the 'infinitive and/or gerund'.

1. _____

2. _____

3. _____

Take turns asking and answering the corrected questions with a partner.

❋ Complete these sentences with a partner. Work together (while speaking out loud).

1. Do you enjoy (go) _____ on a blind date?

2. How do you hope (achieve) _____ a healthy work/life balance?

3. How can you manage (survive/put up with) _____ the yellow dust?

4. Would you think about (wear) _____ couple clothes with your boy/girlfriend?

 Now ask these completed questions to your partner and discuss.

Useful Vocabulary

❋ Try to use all of these words in your discussions today. Check them off as you use each one.

Picky (挑剔的)	Outrageous (粗暴的)	Geek/nerd (书呆子)
Creepy (令人毛骨悚然的)	Pull an all-nighter (熬夜通宵)	Variety shows (综艺节目)
Atmosphere (气氛，大气层)	Personal Hygiene (个人卫生)	Promotion (提升)
Controversial (有争议的)		

Main Activity

❋ Practise asking and answering these questions using the correct grammar.

Ask more follow-up questions (Who/When/Where/Why/What/Which/How…?)

What new skill would you like to learn to do extremely well?

Do you like to shop/shopping online or through TV infomercials (home shopping)?

Would you miss going to bathhouses (sauna/mokyoktang) (桑拿) regularly if you lived overseas?

Do you want to live with your parents until you get married?

I love to watch/watching 'Running Man'? How about you?

* Add 3 relevant and/or common errors from the students' discussion. Correct together and leave the corrected sentences on the board.

1. _____

2. _____

3. _____

* Now, please also correct these sentences with a partner.

1. I will not admit my wife to smoke. Is it a good idea?

_____

2. How long does it take you to wear your make-up?

_____

3. Do you know how to eating spicy food?

_____

4. Have you decided to go to the East Sea (东海) for your vacation?

_____

Take turns asking and answering the corrected questions with a partner.

Pronunciation practice

* Practise the natural English pronunciation of the highlighted words below.

Sink – Think	Some - Thumb	Sin - Thin	Sank you – Thank you	Sing - Thing
Toothpick	Birthday	Healthy	Something	Anything	Athlete
Mass – Math	Tense – Tenth	Mouse – Mouth	Norse – North	Breath	Earth

While studying math on Thursday, I thought 33 was either the third or fourth thing after 30.

Take your thumb out of your mouth. Is there anything you want for your tenth birthday on earth?

I think you are as thin as a toothpick; something unlike a healthy athlete.

More Discussion Questions… (Be sure to ask follow-up questions, also.)

What would happen if someone refused to go to a company dinner (hwaesik)?

Do you hate to watch/watching horror movies?

I don't mind going to K-League (韩国K联赛) soccer games? You?

Could you afford to drink soju (烧酒) in another country?

What time did you usually finish studying each day when you were preparing for your university entrance exam (seuneung)?

Ask students to provide examples from their discussions using the 'useful vocabulary'.

✳ Write 3 more relevant and/or common errors from the students' discussion (on the board). Then correct them together.

1. _____

2. _____

3. _____

✳ Now, please also correct these sentences with a partner.

5. Do you need going to the hospital if you have a runny nose?

_____

6. What things do you often put off to do?

_____

7. Are you planning riding your bike (to cycle/to bike) along the 4-Rivers Cycling Path (sadaeganggil)?

_____

8. Would you prefer to lived in the city or the country?

_____

Take turns asking and answering the corrected questions with your partner.

17. Providing evidence and/or examples

When participating in an academic discussion it is important that you make your ideas clear. This means that when giving your opinion you need to support it with reasons and evidence.

The following language can be used to help you voice your ideas and opinions:

Giving reasons:

- This is due to...
- Because/since...
- Due to the fact that...
- As a result of...
- As a consequence of...
- What I mean by this is (that)...

Giving Evidence:

- For instance...
- For example...
- (Authors name) states that...
- According to (author's name)...
- Statistics from (source) show that...

 Check off each of these expressions when you use them in today's discussion.

❋ Discuss/Debate these topics with your partner or group

- Would you like to go white-water rafting/bungee jumping/skydiving? Why/Why not?
- Do you think Korea should keep following the ideas of Confucianism?

Review   What did we study today? Please provide three examples with correct responses. Say these correct sentences together as a class.

Preview   Please read through the materials for our next class together. Prepare any questions that you may have and we can discuss them in the warm-up session during the next class.

Have a great day. See you next class!

Arrivederci
(ahr-ree-vett-DEHR-chee)

21 I used to love comic books

Previous Class Review

✳ What did we do in the previous lesson?
(Giving advice) Elicit examples from students of:

- target language
- key questions and responses
- relevant vocab
- natural expressions

✳ Write these up on the board and practice them together.
What pronunciation did we work on in the previous
class? (Gerunds/Infinitives). Ask students for some
key examples. Put them on the board and practice
saying them correctly together.

Warm-Up

✳ When do we use 'used to'? Make a sentence using it.
Now make a question. In what situation is it used?

I used to like reading comic books

- I regularly did it in the past
- I don't do it anymore

✳ Students should provide some real-world, personalized examples.

1. _____

2. _____

3. _____

 Now students can open their textbooks and write correct examples from the board in the section above.
Then take turns asking and answering these questions with a partner (ask more follow-up questions).

Language Focus

I used to wear a school uniform (, but now I don't).

我以前穿校服 (但现在不穿)。

What did you use to do?

你以前做什么？

Did you use to cry when you were hungry?

当你饿的时候你有没有哭过？

Where did you use to live?

你过去住在哪里？

I used to live in Daegu. / I've always lived here.

我以前住在大邱。/我一直住在这里。

I didn't use to drink wine(, but now I do).

我过去不喝酒 (但现在喝)。

I used to play the piano.

我过去常弹钢琴。

Yes, I used to cry a lot.

是的，我曾经哭过很多次。

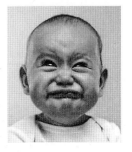

✳ Make 3 other questions with a partner using 'used to'. Then ask these questions to your partner and give the correct response.

1. _____

2. _____

3. _____

✳ Complete these sentences with a partner. Work together (while speaking out loud).

1. I used to eat for free, but now _____

2. When I was in Elementary School, I used to play _____

3. What kind of music did you _____ to listen to?

4. I used to watch _____, but these days I love
watching _____

5. My parents used to _____, but now
_____

 Now say these completed statements to your partner and discuss.

Useful Vocabulary

❋ Try to use all of these words in your discussions today. Check them off as you use each one.

Old school (保守派)

Charming (迷人的)

Grew out of it (增长的)

Keep in touch (保持联系)

Bland (平淡的)

Tipsy (喝醉的)

Allergic to (对...过敏)

Live by myself (独自生活)

Home-made (自制的)

Admire (欣赏)

Troublemaker (麻烦制造者)

Compulsory (强制的，必修的)

Military service (服兵役)

Main Activity

❋ Practise speaking using these questions using the correct grammar (verb tense).

Ask more follow-up questions (Who/When/Where/Why/What/Which/How...?)

Did you use to...

love a celebrity? Who was it?

have a curfew? Do you still have one?

have a teddy bear? Was it as cute as these ones?

study another language (except Korean and English)? Which one?

have a best friend in Middle School? Are they still your best friend?

get in trouble at home/school often when you were young? How about these days?

❋ Add 3 relevant and/or common errors from the students' discussion. Correct together and leave the corrected sentences on the board.

1. _____

2. _____

3. _____

✳ Now, please also correct these sentences with a partner.

1. I use to go to bed before midnight _____

2. Our teacher didn't used to get angry at us. _____

3. I used to go to China last year _____

4. As I know, almost Korean eat many rices for breakfast _____

5. He did used to have played soccer every weekend _____

6. Did you use to wear convenient clothes? _____

7. Most of female student in class used to has princess disease, don't you think?

_____

 Ask and discuss no. 6 & 7 with your partner.

Natural Expressions Practice

✳ Practise the natural English expressions below.

How much time do we have? We have a lot of time.

How many people are currently in Myeong Dong (明洞)?
There are many/lots of people there now.

(General) How many people like tequila? All (100%) /
Almost all (95%) / Most (80%) / Many (60%) / Some
(40%) / Not that many (20%) / Almost no (5%) / No (0%)
people like tequila.

(Specific) How many of the students in our class have
climbed Jirisan (智异山)? All (100%) / Almost all (95%) / Most (80%) / Many (60%) / Some (40%) / Not
that many (20%) / Almost none (5%) / None (0%) of the students in our class have climbed Jirisan.

Generally speaking, how many people like exams / drinking / pizza / winter?

First guess then check the following: (brainstorm more examples)

How many of the students in our class like dancing / living with their parents / singing / soju (烧酒) / sleeping?

More Discussion Questions… (Be sure to ask follow-up questions, also.)

Did you use to have a pet? What was its name?

Who used to be your hero when you were young? Now?

What is a food that you used to hate but now you like?

Did your parents/grandparents use to make their own kimchi (泡菜)? What else?

Did you use to like dressing up as a soldier/princess? How about these days?

My partner didn't use to drink a lot of alcohol, but now…

Did your family use to own a CD and/or DVD player? How about a VHS video player, Walkman, record player?

Ask students to provide examples from their discussions using the 'useful vocabulary'.

✳ Write 3 more relevant and/or common errors from the students' discussion (on the board). Then correct them together.

1. _____

2. _____

3. _____

✳ Now, please also correct these sentences with a partner.

8. Did you use to have small vocabulary? _____

9. When you were a high school, did you use to learn many English grammars?

_____

10. How many family members do you have? _____

11. Where did you use to gone with your High School friends? _____

12. Which sports stars did use to be extremely popular? _____

13. How did people have used to communicate before the internet and cell phones?

_____

 Now ask these completed questions to your partner and discuss.

Critical Thinking & Discussion

18. Giving your opinion more strongly

- I'm absolutely convinced that…

- I'm sure that…

- I strongly believe that…

- I have no doubt that…

- There's no doubt in my mind that…

 Check off each of these expressions when you use them in today's discussion.

✳ Discuss/Debate these topics with your partner or group

- What did your home town use to be like 10 years ago? How about 20/50/100 years ago?

- Compare the differences between how Korea used to be during the Silla Dynasty, and the way it is now.

Review

What did we study today? Please provide three examples with correct responses. Say these correct sentences together as a class.

Preview

Please read through the materials for our next class together. Prepare any questions that you may have and we can discuss them in the warm-up session during the next class.

Have a great day. See you next class!

Previous Class Review

✳ What did we do in the previous lesson?
(Used to) Elicit examples from students of:

- common questions
- natural responses
- relevant vocab

✳ Write these up on the board and practice them together.
What pronunciation/natural expressions did we work on in the previous class? (How much/many). Ask students for some key examples (prompt/ guide them if necessary). Put them on the board and practice saying them correctly together.

Practice these together with a partner for a few minutes.

Warm-Up

✳ When do we use 'Modals of deduction'? Brainstorm the relevant grammar and write it on the board.

- 'Modals of deduction' are used to show possibility, certainly, or impossibility

✳ Get some real-world, personalized examples from students (to be written on the board).

1. _____

2. _____

3. _____

Now students can open their textbooks and write correct examples from the board in the section above.
Then take turns asking and answering these questions with a partner (ask more follow-up questions).

Language Focus

Modals in the Present 情态动词的现在时	Modals in the Past 情态动词的过去时
Possibility 可能性	It may / can / could / might rain. It's cloudy. 可能会下雨。今天多云。 I guess it may / can / could / might have been Lucy on the phone. 我猜可能是露西打来的电话。
Certainty 必然，确实	He has a Rolls Royce. He must be very rich. 他有一辆劳斯莱斯。他一定很富有。 He must have been rich. He had a big house and an expensive car. 他一定很富有。他有一所大房子和一辆昂贵的汽车。
Impossibility (almost) 不可能的（几乎）	He can't be American. His English is terrible. 他不可能是美国人。他的英语很糟糕。 He can't have written that poem. He was illiterate. 他不可能写那首诗。他是文盲。

You mustn't smoke here.
你不能在这里吸烟。

You mustn't have smoked there.
你不该在那里吸烟。

✳ Make (workshop) 3 other questions with a partner using 'modals of deduction'.

1. _____

2. _____

3. _____

> 🎓 Take turns asking these questions to your partner and reply and discuss together.

✳ Complete these sentences with a partner. Work together. (while speaking out loud)

1. You haven't had breakfast! You _____ be hungry, right?

2. You don't look so great. You might _____ drunk a lot last night, yeah?

3. You're South Korean, so you _____ have been to North Korea. Is that right?

4. What shall we do this afternoon. It looks like it _____ rain later?

Now ask these completed questions to your partner and discuss.

Useful Vocabulary

❋ Try to use all of these words in your discussions today. Check them off as you use each one.

Brutal (残酷的)	Cutting-edge (尖端，前沿)	Face-to-face (面对面的)
Cultural awareness (文化意识)	Invested (投资)	

Main Activity

❋ Practise asking and answering these questions using the correct grammar.

Ask more follow-up questions (Who/When/Where/Why/What/Which/How…?)

It must have been easier to make close friends before the internet era, don't you think?

Game of Thrones might be my favourite TV show. How about you?

Do you think that learning some cultural etiquette can be a good way to prepare before traveling?

What could the government have done over the last 20 years to make Korea a better country today?

You can't still be a fan of Starcraft/World of Warcraft (Clash of Clans/League of Legends), can you?

Ask students to provide examples from their discussions using the 'useful vocabulary'.

❋ Add 3 relevant and/or common errors from the students' discussion. Correct together and leave the corrected sentences on the board.

1. _____

2. _____

3. _____

✤ Now, please also correct these sentences with a partner.

1. It must've been difficult to give a birth to Choi Hong-man (崔洪万), hey?

_____

2. You look happy. You have must've moved your house, yeah?

_____

3. I just went in a date with IU (李知恩). You must joking/You can be serious, surely?

_____

4. Do you thinking I can be choosed to play for the Korean national speed-skating team (volleyball/archery)?

_____

 Take turns asking and answering the corrected questions with your partner.

Natural Expressions Practice

✤ Practise the natural English expressions below.

We could've (coulda) won the game if we were fitter, don't you think?

It might've (mighta) been a good idea to bring an umbrella today, right?

It can't've (can'ta) been easy to run a (full) marathon, huh?

I should've (shoulda) gone to bed earlier last night, eh?

If I'd known he liked me, I would've (woulda) asked him out earlier, hey?

If you don't mind me asking, I was wondering if you could tell me: how old you are / if you're married / if you have any children / how tall you are / how much your watch cost / if you're religious / if you've ever taken drugs.

I'm sorry. I'd rather not answer that / That's a bit too personal / That's none of your business.

Solve the mystery

Last night, Sherlock Kim (夏洛克 金) was walking home when she saw a man stumble out of an apartment building clutching his chest and fall down dead on the side of the road. He had been stabbed in the heart with a dagger (knife)! Sherlock investigated the apartment building and found that only 1 person lived on each of the 5 floors and there was no-one else in the building. Each resident had a different name, nationality, age, weapon, and reason (motive) to want to kill the victim, Mr. Moriarty Lee. Gather the relevant information (clues) and help Sherlock solve the case.

 Prepare the information for this activity from the second last page of this unit.

❋ Write 3 more relevant and/or common errors from the students' discussion (on the board). Then correct them together.

1. _____

2. _____

3. _____

❋ Now, please also correct these sentences with a partner.

5. I should've studied as possible as I can, right? _____

6. You are very kindly. You must've made a very nice boyfriend.

_____

7. I have to buy something at super. Can I lend 10 dollar?

_____

8. Nice to meet you again. Actually, we must've met before, right?

_____

 Take turns asking and answering the corrected questions with your partner.

Critical Thinking & Discussion

19. Persuading/Changing opinions

- I am certain ...
- I'm sure that you can see that ...
- What needs to be done/what we need to do ...
- I ask you to think about ...
- I say this in order to ...
- Nevertheless ...
- On the other hand ...
- It has come to my attention that ...
- If you move forward with ...
- Surely ...
- If [ ] were to happen, then ...
- Although it may seem ...

- Obviously ...
- Regardless ...
- This can be fixed by ...

 Check off each of these expressions when you use them in today's discussion.

✳ Discuss/Debate these topics with your partner or group

- What do you think is a great way the world might/could have acted in the past to avoid terrorism these days?
- Where do you think might/could be a good place to travel to broaden your horizons?

Review

What did we study today? Please provide three examples with correct responses. Say these correct sentences together as a class.

Preview

Please read through the materials for our next class together. Prepare any questions that you may have and we can discuss them in the warm-up session during the next class.

Have a great day. See you next class!

It's a good idea to pre-teach the following expressions/vocabulary before starting the activity!

| Blackmail | Creature | Inherit | Lethal (deadly) | Villain |

Be sure to speak with your partner consistently during this activity. Practice using the expressions we have learned in this unit (modals of deduction), i.e. 'Darth Vader might be…', 'Gollum can't have…', 'The killer must be…!' etc.

Floor	Name	Age	Nationality	Weapon	Motive
5th					
4th					
3rd					
2nd					
1st					

✳ Write down all of the clues in the section provided below and then work together to figure out who killed Moriarty, by filling in the information in the grid above.

Don't forget to practice speaking as you explain each deduction to your partner (and yourself)! Good luck!

1. _____

2. _____

3. _____

4. _____

5. _____

6. _____

7. _____

8. _____

9. _____

10. _____

11. _____

12. _____

* Photocopy these clues and cut them into separate strips. Put them on a table at the front of the classroom. Then ask students to take turns coming up and taking 1 clue and telling that information to their partner (either memorise or use and return).

Gollum is from Middle Earth and lives on the top floor

Moriarty was blackmailing his ex-lover, Dracula, aged 212

Frankenstein lives on the third floor

The 41-year-old lives one floor below the creature from Middle Earth

Voldermort, who is 55 years old, lives one floor below the 212-year old

The American man's name is Darth Vader

The German is only 3 years old

The Romanian man has deadly sharp teeth

The 596-year-old wanted to inherit a magic ring from Moriarty and lives one floor above the man with the light-saber

The creature with gigantic lethal fists was jealous of Moriarty and lives one floor below the American

The English villain hated Moriarty because he was a rival in evil

The man who wanted revenge against Moriarty lives one floor below the man with the killer fish

Solution

Name	Age	Nationality	Weapon	Motive
Gollum	596	Middle Earth	Killer fish	Inheritance
Darth Vader	41	American	Light-saber	Revenge
Frankenstein	3	German	Fists	Jealousy
Dracula	212	Romanian	Teeth	Blackmail
Voldermort	55	English		Rival

This is all of the available information. What can you deduce from this? What information is missing? Why? Remember back to the introduction to the story – 'saw a man stumble out of an apartment building clutching his chest and fall down dead on the side of the road. He had been stabbed in the heart!'

What is the missing weapon and where is it? Therefore, who is the killer?

The missing weapon is Voldermort's knife (dagger), which he must've used to stab Moriarty Lee. It is still in Moriarty's chest. Therefore, Voldermort is the killer.

Find the murderer! Good luck, Sherlocks!

23 We were robbed!

Previous Class Review

❊ What did we do in the previous lesson?
(Modals of deduction)
Elicit examples from students of:

- common questions
- natural responses
- relevant vocab

❊ Write these up on the board and practice them together.
What pronunciation/natural expressions did we work on in the
previous class? (Modals of deduction). Ask students for some key
examples (prompt/guide them if necessary). Put them on the board
and practice saying them correctly together.

 Practice these together with a partner for a few minutes.

Warm-Up

❊ When do we use 'the passive'? Brainstorm the relevant grammar and write it on the board.

- 'The passive' is used when the subject of the action is:
  - Not known to the speaker
  - Not as important as the object

❊ Get some real-world, personalized examples from students (to be written on the board).

1. _____

2. _____

3. _____

 Now students can open their textbooks and write correct examples from the board in the section above.
Then take turns asking and answering these questions with a partner (ask more follow-up questions).

Language Focus

Active:
主动态；

Mr. Potter teaches Magic 101.
波特先生教魔术101.

Shakespeare wrote 'Romeo and Juliet'.
莎士比亚写了'罗密欧与朱丽叶'.

The simple present:
一般现在时：

The newspaper is delivered at 7am.
报纸在早上7点被送来。

Are the classrooms cleaned once a week?
教室每周打扫一次吗？

Present Continuous
现在进行时

Sorry, I can't talk – I'm being pushed (shoved) around on the subway.
对不起，我不能说话。-- 我正在地铁上被推来推去。

Have you ever been dumped on Valentine's Day? 你有没有在情人节被甩过？

Simple Future
一般将来时

Do you think you'll be expelled from school/ uni if you get caught selling drugs?
如果你被抓到贩卖毒品，你会被学校开除吗？

I'm going to be fired if I tell my boss what I think. 如果我告诉老板我的想法，我会被炒鱿鱼的。

Passive using by:
被动态使用by：

Magic 101 is taught by Mr. Potter.
魔术101由波特先生教。

'Romeo and Juliet' was written by Shakespeare.
罗密欧与朱丽叶是莎士比亚写的。

The simple past:
一般过去时：

The university was founded in 1895.
这所大学成立于1895年。

Was your apartment renovated last year?
你的公寓去年翻修了吗？

Present Perfect
现在完成时

Future Continuous
将来进行时

* Make (workshop) 3 other questions with a partner using 'the passive'.

1. _____

2. _____

3. _____

Take turns asking these questions to your partner and reply and discuss together.

* Complete these sentences with a partner. Work together (while speaking out loud).

1. What's wrong with the toilet? _____ it broken?

2. What would your Dad do if he _____ hired by Google?

3. How do you feel when you _____ being interviewed?

Now ask these completed questions to your partner and discuss.

4. Do you know about any famous people who have _____ arrested?

Useful Vocabulary

✳ Try to use all of these words in your discussions today. Check them off as you use each one.

Capital punishment (死刑) Be held (举行) Dynasty (王朝) Pricey (昂贵的)

Addictive (上瘾的) Harvest Moon Festival (Korean Thanksgiving – Chuseok) (中秋节)

Main Activity

✳ Practise asking and answering these questions using the correct grammar.

Ask more follow-up questions (Who/When/Where/Why/What/Which/How...?)

When was Hangeul (韩文) created?

Who are the most expensive cars in Korea made by?

Do you think you are going to be punished, if you come to class late?

Which cell phone game has been played the most in Korea?

When and where will the next Olympic games be held?

When was the last time you saw a Korean ancestral ceremony (祭祀) being performed?

Ask students to provide examples from their discussions using the 'useful vocabulary'.

✳ Add 3 relevant and/or common errors from the students' discussion. Correct together and leave the corrected sentences on the board.

1. _____

2. _____

3. _____

✽ Now, please also correct these sentences with a partner.

1. When was the last time you was shocked? _____

2. Do you think you are gone to be kicked out of class, if you smoke here?

   _____

3. Do you think my phone will be stealing at the bathhouse (mokyoktang)?

   _____

4. Do you know the last time a person was execution in Korea?

   _____

5. How do you think Kim, Jong Eun's (金正云) next birthday would be celebrated?

   _____

 Take turns asking and answering the corrected questions with your partner.

Pronunciation practice

✽ Practise the natural English pronunciation of the highlighted words below.

Tricky pronunciation:

I wonder whether that woman would prefer wood or wool for her wounded wolf?

To keep your blood warm during a flood, you should choose nice food and a good book.

How many syllables in the following word? –   S T R E T C H E D

Say the following numbers – 4,372   1,729,568   2.56   ¾

Quiz Time

 Make ~5 Qs with a partner then each pair should ask 1 question (go around the class) per round. Keep the score on the board and choose a suitable prize for the winner (or mild punishment for the loser). Good luck!

✽ Make your own questions using:

Make your own questions using:

What was written/directed/composed/sung/designed/built/
made/painted/created/held/discovered/invented

by…?

✳ Write 3 more relevant and/or common errors from the students' discussion (on the board). Then correct them together.

1. _____

2. _____

3. _____

✳ Now, please also correct these sentences with a partner.

6. He was died by cancer _____

7. My leg was sick _____

8. The concert is finish _____

9. When was your older sibling/mother graduated from university?

_____

10. Have you ever been contacted by a Nigerian prince?

_____

11. What do you feel this morning? _____

12. How many years ago did was Park, Chung Hee (朴正熙) dead?

_____

13. Who was 'The Vegetarian' (《素食者》) writing by?

_____

Take turns asking and answering the corrected questions with a partner.

Critical Thinking & Discussion

20. Wrapping up a discussion

- Keep to the committed ending time, unless you ask the group if they would like to continue for a specified period of time.
- Summarize (or have a participant summarize) the major points of the discussion:
  - The major points of agreement and disagreement, if appropriate.
  - Issues that were discussed but not resolved.
- Comment on (or have the group comment on) how the discussion went:
- How do participants feel about their own participation?
- What was good about the discussion and what could have been better?
- Did people feel free to express their opinions?
- Do they have suggestions for better facilitation?
- If appropriate, help the group decide what the next steps should be (if any).
- Thank everyone for the discussion; for their honest participation, etc.

 Check off each of these when you use them in today's discussion.

❊ Discuss/Debate these topics with your partner or group

- What are the most impressive landmarks ever built?
- What's the most interesting book written by Shin Kyung-Sook (申京淑)?

Review

What did we study today? Please provide three examples with correct responses. Say these correct sentences together as a class.

Preview

Please read through the materials for our next class together. Prepare any questions that you may have and we can discuss them in the warm-up session during the next class.

Have a great day. See you next class!  Goodbye

24 Around the world

Previous Class Review

✳ What did we do in the previous 5 units?
   Elicit examples from students of:

   - common questions
   - natural responses
   - relevant vocab

✳ Write these up on the board and practice them together.
   What pronunciation/natural expressions did we work on in the previous 5 units? Ask students for some key examples (prompt/guide them if necessary). Put them on the board and practice saying them correctly together.

 Practice these together with a partner for a few minutes.

Warm-Up

✳ Where have you traveled? Which place was your favorite? Where would you really love to go?

✳ Get some real-world, personalized examples from students (to be written on the board).

1. _____

2. _____

3. _____

 Now students can open their textbooks and write correct examples from the board in the section above. Then take turns discussing these statements with a partner (ask more follow-up questions).

Language Focus

Where have you been?   Where would you like to go?

What are some great things to see and do there?

What are some interesting local foods and/or drinks to try there?

Do you know some comfortable and affordable places to stay?

What's the weather like there?

Do you have any useful language tips before going there?

Are there any other interesting places to visit nearby?

Can you recommend any local products that would be good souvenirs or gifts?

How much should I expect to pay for different things there; transport, food etc?

✳ Make 3 other questions related to travel.

1. _____

2. _____

3. _____

> 🎓 Take turns asking these questions to your partner and reply and discuss together.

✳ Complete these sentences with a partner. Work together. (while speaking out loud)

1. If I _____ to Paris, what should I do there?

2. Do you like to go (travel) _____ alone?

3. Which place/s did you used _____ visit often when you were young?

4. You must've _____ to Jeju-do, right?

5. Were you (exhaust) _____ after you came back from your package tour around South America?

> 🎓 Now ask these completed questions to your partner and discuss.

Useful Vocabulary

✳ Try to use all of these words in your discussions today. Check them off as you use each one.

    Layover/stopover (短暂的停留)   Scuba diving (水肺潜水)   Adventurous (爱冒险的)

    Globetrotter (环球旅行者)   Ex-pat (海外国民)   Nuclear power (核能)

    Relatively close (相对封闭)   Package tour (跟团游)   Working holiday (工作假期)

    Travel bug (旅游癖)

Main Activity

✳ Practice asking and answering these questions using the correct grammar.

Ask more follow-up questions (Who/When/Where/Why/What/Which/How…?)

Is there a place that you used to want to visit, but not anymore?

Where would you love to go?

If you could travel non-stop for 3 years, would you?

You can't have been to more than 10 different countries already, right?

What's the next foreign country that you might visit? When do you think you might go there?

✳ Add 3 relevant and/or common errors from the students' discussion. Correct together and leave the corrected sentences on the board.

1. _____

2. _____

3. _____

✳ Now, please also correct these sentences with a partner.

1. If you have an early flight at a.m. 8 and a half, what time should you get up?

_____

2. I didn't used to enjoy flying, but now I love it. You? _____

3. Do you like going to overseas/abroad? _____

4. According to my opinion, you can't have been to Morocco. Right?

_____

 Take turns asking and answering the corrected questions with a partner.

Natural Expressions/Pronunciation Practice

❊ Practise the natural English expressions and pronunciation of the highlighted words below.

What do you prepare for/believe in/approve of/concentrate on/talk about/ listen to/agree with?

That thing you think is the third theme I've heard, so thanks for your truthful thoughts.

How many of the teachers at this university/school are geniuses?

Who coulda been a better leader that mighta made life in Korea easier?

Would a good woman choose to help a bloodied, wounded wolf get food during a flood?

More Discussion Questions… (Be sure to ask follow-up questions, also.)

Would you consider living overseas for the rest of your life? If not, then for how long?

Have you ever been stuck at an airport for hours because your flight was delayed?

Which place do you really hope to visit one day?

Did you use to travel a lot when you were growing up?

If you live in another country for a while, will you try as many new experiences as possible?

 Ask students to provide examples from their discussions using the 'useful vocabulary'.

✻ Write 3 more relevant and/or common errors from the students' discussion (on the board). Then correct them together.

1. _____

2. _____

3. _____

✻ Now, please also correct these sentences with a partner .

5. If you could live at foreign country, which country would you choose?

_____

6. You might be gone Japan, yeah? _____

7. Who were planes inventing by? _____

8. If going trip London 3 weeks, what would be the cost?

_____

 Take turns asking and answering the corrected questions with your partner.

Presentation Topics

- If you could change the Korean education system, how would you improve it?

- What are the main things you hope to achieve during your working life?

- What didn't use to be important in the world when you were born, but is now?

- What might have been the most useful advice you've ever been given? Why?

- What was invented this millennium that has had a significant impact on the world?

Writing Test (optional):

Write 10 to 15 sentences about one of the topics above.

Presentation

Read carefully through your writing activity after you have checked the grammar with your teacher. Give a short presentation (1 to 2 minutes) about this to your partner or classmates. Ask if there are any questions and discuss further.

Review

What did we study today? Please provide three examples with correct responses. Say these correct sentences together as a class.

Preview

Please read through the materials for our next class together. Prepare any questions that you may have and we can discuss them in the warm-up session during the next class.

Have a great day. See you next class!

Goodbye.
I'll miss
you

ANSWERS

1. Are you crazy?

1. **Are** you busy these days? Why?
2. **Do** your friends like to drink makkeoli on rainy days?
3. You don't wanna go out tonight? **Yes**, I do / No, I **don't**.
4. **Does** your friend want to join us for dinner?
5. **Are** you are good at playing pool (pocketball)?

1. Are you confident when you speak in front of other people?
2. Are you bored when you watch romantic movies?
3. Did you lose weight?
4. Doesn't your best friend have a part-time job?
5. Are you comfortable when you play with your friends?
6. Did you get a haircut?
7. Is your home near here?
8. Do you like cats?
9. Do you know my opinion (what I think)?

2. What's going on?

1. **What do you think** is the best genre of music?
2. **Where in the world** would you love to visit?
3. **When does the cherry blossom season** start and finish in Korea?
4. **Who is your favorite** movie star?
5. **Why do parents stick** Korean candy (yeot) out the front of High School's on their kid's University Entrance Exam (Seunul) day?
6. **Which kind of seafood** do you enjoy the most?
7. **How are you feeling** today?
8. **How often do you go** to a sauna (bathhouse)?
9. **How much homework** do you usually do each day?
10. **How many people** live in Daejeon?

1. When do most people have free time?
2. How tall would you like be?
3. What do you think (How do you feel) about living in Korea?
4. I don't know what the problem is. Do you?

3. How often do you sing to yourself?

1. **How often** do you travel to another city/town?
2. **I often** check the daily news. How about you?
3. **How often** do you play drinking games?

1. Do you sometimes sing to yourself?
2. I rarely travel to (take a trip to) another country. Do you?
3. Do you often go home using public transport?
4. How often are you drunk and throw up? / How often do you get drunk and throw up?
5. How often do you go on a blind date or have a group meeting?
6. How often do you travel (take a trip) overseas/abroad/to another country?
7. How often do you ask a question to your teacher?

4. What will you do on your vacation?

1. How **will you celebrate** after you finish your exams?
2. **What will your family do** for the next Chuseok holidays?
3. **Will you read** a book today?
4. What **time will you probably go** home today?
5. **Will you have** dinner with your parents tonight?
6. Which team **will win** the next Soccer (Football) World Cup? **Who might be** the star player?

1. Will you meet (Are you meeting) your friends tonight?
2. Will you graduate from your university in 3 months?
3. When might you find a girlfriend/boyfriend?
4. Will you go to the library after class?
5. Do you think your friend will marry his girlfriend?
6. Where will you hang out with your friends on the weekend?
7. Will you be absent from class tomorrow?
8. Where might you go on vacation next summer?

5. Do you want to go home?

1. **Do you want me to** bring you some beer?
2. Where **do you want to go** after class?
3. What **do you want to** have for dinner?
4. What kind of husband/wife **do you want to** have?

1. Do you want to live in the country?
2. Don't you want your brother to remain single for his whole life?

3. Do you want to see alien life arrive on earth?
4. Do you want to go bowling this weekend?
5. Do you want to listen to music?
6. How much money do you want to make?
7. Do you want to climb a mountain (go hiking) after class?
8. Do you want to go shopping later?
9. Do you want some chicken?

6. Mmm, this is tasty!

1. **How often** do you eat bibimbap?
2. **What will** you have for dinner tonight?
3. What **do you want to** drink when you eat chicken?

1. How many times have you thrown up when you were drunk (drinking)?
2. What do you think (How do you feel) about having pizza for breakfast?
3. Does one of your friends want to lose weight?
4. How often do you get together with (meet) your sister?
5. Will eating a lot of meat make kids (get) taller?
6. What do you want to eat when you are hungover (sukjae issoyo)?
7. When will you not eat for more than 12 hours?
8. Is there a McDonalds near here (nearby)?
9. What's your favorite dish at Chinese restaurants?

7. What are you thinking about?

1. What **are you doing** right now?
2. Who do you know that **is always complaining**?
3. What other subjects **are you studying** these days?
4. Where **are you doing** immediately after class?

1. Are you working on an assignment at the moment?
2. Are you still working at your part-time job?
3. Why are you forever arguing with me?
4. What sort of music are teenagers listening to these days?
5. I'm thinking about contacting G-Dragon. Should I?
6. What are you wearing?
7. These days, more people are using Facebook Messenger than texting? Do you agree?
8. Do you think your English is improving?
9. Why are you always smiling?
10. What will you be doing on the weekend?

8. What did you do last summer?

1. **My brother watched** TV for 5 hours straight yesterday?
2. **Did you buy** anything on the weekend?
3. **Did you know** how to swim when you were 10 years old?
4. **Were you awake** at midnight last night?

1. Did you look at the subway timetable this morning?
2. What time did you come back home last night?
3. Did you play Starcraft when you were young?
4. When's the last time you swam in the ocean?
5. Did you catch a cold (Do you have a cold)?
6. Did you eat jajangmyeon yesterday?
7. Were you drunk last night?
8. Did you throw up and black out (lose your memory)?
9. Did you do yoga in 2016?
10. What did you do last weekend?
11. I met her two weeks ago

9. Take it easy!

1. Take medicine!
2. Drink faster (more quickly)!
3. Lend me (Let me borrow) ₩10,000, please.
4. Listen to your mother!
5. Don't tease me!
6. Go home!
7. Careful not to make a mistake.
8. Always do your best!
9. See you next time!
10. I dropped my phone into the toilet. How stupid (am I)!
11. (To be honest), please sign here!

10. What are you gonna do tonight?

1. **Are you going to** play badminton this evening?
2. After I retire, **I'm going to** live in the countryside. How about you?
3. Are you **going to have** a hard time sleeping tonight after drinking 3 coffees?
4. I'm so tired. I think I'm **going to** go to bed early tonight. You?

1. Are you going to get a haircut soon?
2. Who are/aren't you gonna go dancing with (in Hongdae/ Gangnam etc) this Friday night?

3. Are you gonna review this lesson at home tonight?

4. Which famous restaurant are you gonna go to this month?

5. Why are we gonna pay separately at dinner tonight?

6. I'm gonna go straight home and sleep

7. Why are/aren't you gonna eat dog food at the start of next summer?

8. Are you gonna study hard next class?

9. Are you gonna get married in the next 10 years?

11. We're on vacation in 3 weeks

1. Where are you **gonna go after class**?

2. I have to **finish my assignment by 4pm on Monday.**

3. I'm **going** to Seokcho **next Thursday**, but I'll **come back 3 days later.**

4. I'm really looking forward to **going to Guam in 2 months.** How long will you stay there? I'll **stay there for 5 days.**

5. I **have a yoga class at 11am tomorrow** and I will **stay there until 2pm. After the class** I will really do my best.

6. **In August** I'm going to China. I have to **prepare my visa within the next 6 weeks.**

1. I will go to my hometown in 2 weeks

2. We should complete our homework by p.m. 6 on Friday, right?

3. I'm gonna stay at my brother's house for 2 weeks

4. I have a flight to catch on Wednesday at 10pm

5. Did you have breakfast in the morning on the weekend?

6. Do you plan to meet your boy/girlfriend at 7pm on Friday?

7. Do you plan to meet your friends in the Summer vacation?

8. Would you like to get married to a celebrity in 5 years?

12. Do you wanna hang out on the weekend?

1. When you're **feeling down** what do you do to **cheer yourself up**?

2. Do you prefer to **stand out** in a crowd, or would you rather **blend in**?

3. Who do you **take after** the most; your mom or your dad?

4. Do you think that **capital punishment** should be **done away with**?

1. You look stressed! How can you put up with that? Don't give up!

2. Calm down! You can do it! Hang in there! Harden up!

3. How often do you go out with your friends?

4. What are some of your favorite places to hang out?

5. Does Hye-soo plan to get married in 2 years with her celebrity (famous) partner (fiancé)?

6. Have you ever fallen out with a friend or relative?

7. When you're worn out, what's a good pick-me-up?

8. What's a shocking surprise that you found out about a famous person?

9. Do you want to go shopping later?

13. This is so exciting. I'm thrilled

1. I once fell over on the subway; I was so **embarrassed.** Tell me an embarrassing story?

2. Have you heard any **shocking** scandals recently. Why were you shocked?

3. I think Gyro-drop at Lotte World is **frightening.** When have you felt frightened?

4. That stingray (hongeo) smells disgusting? When do you feel **disgusted** by food?

1. I'm really bored. I have nothing to do. You?

2. Are you satisfied with your textbook?

3. When do you feel exhausted?

4. What do you think about Bollywood movies?

5. Music videos make me very entertained?

6. He was so rude. I was (felt) insulted

7. Hiking is very tiring

8. That show is not interesting to me

9. It's very irritating to me

10. She is funny/amusing (She makes me amused)

11. I'm not satisfied with the dinner

12. Modern art is not fascinating

13. An international traveler asked me a question on the street and I couldn't speak English well, so I felt so embarrassed/frustrated/disappointed

14. What should I have for dinner?

1. I know someone who sometimes drives after drinking. **He'd better** stop doing that. Any suggestions?

2. My partner sends so many Kakao Talk messages during class. **If I were her, I'd.....**

3. My brother's not very healthy, these days. **What should he do?**

4. **You ought to** think seriously before changing your degree. Don't you think?
5. **The taxi driver has to (must)** stop at the red light. Do you always agree?
6. The bar is totally out of beer and soju. **Why don't** we try some...? / **We could always** try some...

1. I just threw up! I'd better to go to a medical clinic, right?
2. What kind of person should I marry?
3. Where's the most relaxing place to talk with your friends?
4. Your dog stinks! Why don't you wash him?
5. What must I bring to the end-of-semester exam?
6. Personally, I'm nervous when I give presentations. You?
7. This dress doesn't fit/suit me. Any tips?
8. I need to get from Uijeongbu to Gimpo airport in 90 minutes. What the best way?
9. How much helpful advice could you give to a Korean High School student?
10. What should you say about Korean food which non-Koreans are not familiar with?
11. How should I get to Mokpo? Sorry, I'm not (exactly) sure.

15. I am the greatest!

1. What is **the scariest** move you have **ever** seen?
2. Which is **more exciting/boring**, classical music or trot?
3. Who is **the sexiest** person in the world?
4. Soju is **better/stronger/tastier/than** beer, huh?
5. **The most dangerous** person in the world is **me**

1. Do you think summer is better than winter?
2. Is your brother crazier than your sister?
3. Don't you think Disneyland is more exciting than Wolmido?
4. Is Bill Gates richer than Lee, Kun-hee?
5. I like you so much, don't you think?
6. Is Barcelona the most amazing place you've ever visited?
7. Who is the craziest person you know?
8. Is Myeong-dong the busiest place in Seoul?
9. Hallasan is the highest mountain in Korea, right?
10. Who's favorite hobby is chasing lots of Korean women?

16. Have you ever talked to a celebrity?

1. **Have you ever sung** an English song at a singing room?
2. **I have seen** the movie, 'About Time'. How about you?
3. How many times **have you drunk** soju?
4. **Have you been** late for this class? Why/Why not?
5. What is the strangest food that **you have ever eaten**?
6. **Have you ever seen** a K-pop star in real life? Who was it? Where?

1. Have you ever ridden on a roller-coaster?
2. Yes, I've ridden on a roller-coaster. You?
3. No, I have never ridden on a roller-coaster
4. Last year, I went to Everland
5. I have been to Brazil where I met many interesting people. You?
6. I have (never) eaten frog's legs. Is it true?
7. Did you see the news yesterday?
8. Have you ever been to Australia?

17. What were you thinking?

1. While I **was playing** on my computer last night, the internet dropped out. How do you think I felt?
2. I **was studying** almost around the clock when I was a High School student. Do you think that's healthy?
3. My friend **was** always **working** overtime at his last company. Is that common?
4. They **were practising** piano every day when they were young? Was that useful?

1. Were you playing with your phone, while you were waiting for this class to start?
2. Have you ever hurt yourself, while you were snowboarding/water-skiing etc?
3. Did you get any pop-up ads while you were playing with your computer recently? Change text book
4. Have you ever fallen asleep, when you were sitting in a class?
5. When did you last shout while you were listening to music using earphones?
6. Did you check out your phone while you were talking to someone recently?
7. When's the last time you fell asleep while you were traveling on the subway? Change text book
8. He told me he wasn't feeling well?
9. (Personally), I was dancing at 11 p.m. last night. You?

18. Were you checking out the amazing movie?

1. Do you think **predictable** or **innovative** movies are **more** interesting?
2. What movie would you tell your friends that **they'd better** see?
3. What's **the most confusing** movie you've ever seen?
4. We **were watching** a movie when I dropped my phone into my popcorn. **Have you ever done** that?

1. Do you feel irritated when you get off a bus at the wrong stop?
2. In my opinion, you ought to take the KTX. Do you agree?
3. Is Park, Geun Hye smarter than her father?
4. Have you ever traveled (taken a trip) to Europe?
5. Were you eating chicken in your kitchen last night?
6. My favorite hobby is listening to music and playing computer game. You?
7. Have you ever drunk 4 bottles of soju?
8. Have you been a member of staff at a company?
9. Why don't you practice English every day?
10. Were you excited to find out that Ji-ae is single?
11. I was really looking forward to this class? You?
12. Where's the most interesting place to go in Seoul for window shopping?
13. What should I do if I lose my bag on the subway?
14. We should wrap this up now. Is that ok?

19. If I were the queen, I'd...?

1. **If I finish** my homework early, I'll go out tonight? You?
2. **If you drink** vodka till 3am, **you feel** terrible the next day, right?
3. Where **would you** live, **if you could** live anywhere in the world?
4. **If your apartment was** on fire, what are the first 3 things **you should/would** save?

1. If I was 24, how many years before you think I should get a job/married?
2. If I said, 'Konnichiwa!', would you understand?
3. If you lived near your school/office, it would be very convenient, eh?
4. If you take medicine every day, will you be healthy?

5. If shops have customers and hotels have guests, will the owners be happy?
6. If you could choose to have any job, what would it be?
7. If you are crazy about soccer, what should you do?
8. How would you feel if you met many international people at the same time alone?

20. Do you like to go drinking?

1. Do you **enjoy going** on a blind date?
2. How do you **hope to achieve** a healthy work/life balance?
3. How can you **manage to put up with** the yellow dust?
4. Would you **think about wearing** couple clothes with your boy/girlfriend?

1. I will not allow my wife to smoke. Is that a good idea?
2. How long does it take you to put on your make-up?
3. Can you/Do you like to eat spicy food?
4. Have you decided to go to the East Sea on your vacation?
5. Do you need to go to a medical clinic/ Do you need to see a doctor if you have a runny nose?
6. What things do you often put off doing?
7. Are you planning to ride your bike along the 4-Rivers Cycling Path (sadaeganggil)?
8. Would you prefer to live in the city or the country?

21. I used to love comic books

1. I **used to** eat for free, but now I have to buy my own food.
2. When I was in Elementary School, **I used to** play games with my friends every day.
3. What kind of music did you **use to** listen to?
4. I **used to** watch cartoons, but these days I love watching documentaries.
5. My parents **used to** live in Busan, but now they live in Seoul.

1. I used to go to bed before midnight.
2. Our teacher didn't use to get angry at us.
3. I used to go to China often / I went to China last year.
4. As you know, most Koreans eat a lot of rice for breakfast.
5. He used to play soccer every weekend.

6. Did you use to wear comfortable clothes?
7. Most of the female students in our class used to have princess syndrome, don't you think?
8. Did you use to have a small vocabulary?
9. When you were a high school student (in high school), did you use to learn a lot of English grammar?
10. How many people are there in your family?
11. Where did you use to go with your High School friends?
12. Which sports stars used to be extremely popular?
13. How did people use to communicate before the internet and cell phones?

22. I could've been a contender!

1. You haven't had breakfast! **You must be hungry**, right?
2. You don't look so great. **You might have drunk** a lot last night, yeah?
3. You're South Korean, so **you can't have been** to North Korea. Is that right?
4. What shall we do this afternoon. It looks like **it might rain** later?

1. It must've been difficult to give birth to Choi Hong-man, hey?
2. You look happy. You must've moved, yeah?
3. I just went on a date with IU. You must be joking/You can't be serious, surely?
4. Do you thinking I can be chosen to play for the Korean national speed-skating team (volleyball/archery)?
5. I should've studied as hard/much as I could (as hard/much as possible), right?
6. You are very kind. You must've found a very nice boyfriend.
7. I have to buy something at the corner (local) shop. Can I borrow (Can you lend me) 10 dollars?
8. Nice to meet you again. Actually, we might've met before, right?

23. We were robbed!

1. What's wrong with the toilet? **Is it broken**?
2. What would your Dad do if **he was hired** by Google?
3. How do you feel when **you are being interviewed**?
4. Do you know about any famous people **who have been arrested**?

1. When was the last time you were shocked?
2. Do you think you are going to be kicked out of class, if you smoke here?
3. Do you think my phone will be stolen at the bathhouse (mokyoktang)?
4. Do you know the last time a person was executed in Korea?
5. How do you think Kim, Jong Eun's next birthday will be celebrated?
6. He died of cancer
7. My leg was sore (injured)
8. The concert has finished
9. When did your older sibling/mother graduate from university?
10. Have you ever been contacted by a Nigerian prince? Change in textbook
11. How do you feel this morning?
12. How many years ago did Park, Chung Hee die (was PCH killed)?
13. Who was 'The Vegetarian' written by?

24. Around the world

1. **If I go** to Paris, what should I do there?
2. Do you like **to go traveling** alone?
3. Which place/s did you **used to visit** often when you were young?
4. You **must've been** to Jeju-do, right?
5. **Were you exhausted** after you came back from your package tour around South America?

1. If you have an early flight at 8.30a.m. (half past 8 in the morning), what time should you get up?
2. I didn't use to enjoy flying, but now I love it. You?
3. Do you like going overseas/abroad?
4. (In my opinion), you can't have been to Morocco. Right?
5. If you could live in a foreign country, which country would you choose?
6. You might have been to Japan, yeah?
7. Who were planes invented by?
8. If you're (I'm) going on a trip to London in 3 weeks, how much would it cost?

ENGLISH FOR CHINESE SPEAKERS

초판 1쇄 인쇄　2019년 1월 10일
초판 1쇄 발행　2019년 1월 15일

저　자	Greg Dawson
펴낸이	임 순 재
펴낸곳	**(주)한올출판사**
등　록	제11-403호
주　소	서울시 마포구 모래내로 83(성산동 한올빌딩 3층)
전　화	(02) 376-4298(대표)
팩　스	(02) 302-8073
홈페이지	www.hanol.co.kr
e-메일	hanol@hanol.co.kr
ISBN	979-11-5685-736-5